Fundemic
Moments

Life is way too serious—especially for us immigrants who work hard for our money and to become the best as we suffer silently and serve with a smile. To exacerbate our challenges, the news and talk around the pandemic has pushed us to madness. But that's only true if you've lost your Pinoy way!

In true Filipino fashion, *Fundemic Moments* injects levity, lifting the corner of my frown much like Botox. Somehow, Romeo Honorio has captured my thoughts and centrifuged them to get just the right dose of pun as the best cure for COVID. But laughter isn't always as easy as swallowing a pill.

I'm so thrilled Romeo has written this book, his third. I feel like we share the same Pinoy punny bone. You'll enjoy it! Even though my Puti husband and Mestizo kids have a hard time getting me, I know they'll enjoy it too. This book encapsulates laughter as the best medicine for any virus or the blues. Take the red pill!

—Astrid Kuhn Ph.D., Social Scientist, Calgary, Alberta

Fundemic Moments is a powerful resource that will help you discover the other side of the pandemic times! Great source of chuckles and laughter.

—Abby Villanueva, President and CEO, A G & Associates, Calgary, Alberta

Stories are stored memories. No matter how good or bad, jolly or melancholy, as long as it's Romeo's story, you can always find ingenuity. What can't be technically defined can always be described, as proven by the unique presentation that captures the modern-contemporary vocabulary to fully appreciate that life is a gift to be enjoyed and not a problem to be solved. Fun-filled annotations and artistic methodology are fun-tastically displayed in this prose. By reading its printed pages, you will grow intellectually and not only in age.

—Lito Mendoza Velasco, Editor-in-Chief, *Alberta Filipino Journal*

Romeo Honorio's third book, *Fundemic Moments*, gives a humorous yet insightful understanding of the last few years of life journeying through the global pandemic. Romeo's simple yet profound thoughts allow you into the personal and intimate journey of a man who loves his family, friends, and his God while not taking himself too seriously. You'll be laughing at one moment, reflecting personally at another moment, and constantly learning a value that you need to apply to your own life. This is a book you need to read!

—Matt Wilks, Pastor and Author, *Cultivate: A Youth Worker's Guide to Establishing Healthy Relationships*

Fundemic Moments

Moments

Pandemic Chuckles Unmasked

ROMEO HONORIO

FUNDEMIC MOMENTS
Copyright © 2023 by Romeo Honorio

Scripture quotations marked (NIV) are taken from the Holy Bible, NEW INTERNATIONAL VERSION®, NIV® Copyright © 1973, 1978, 1984, 2011 by Biblica, Inc.® Used by permission. All rights reserved worldwide. • Scripture quotations marked (AMPC) are taken from the Amplified® Bible, Copyright © 1954, 1958, 1962, 1964, 1965, 1987 by The Lockman Foundation. Used by permission. lockman.org.

ISBN: 978-1-4866-2458-4
eBook ISBN: 978-1-4866-2459-1

Word Alive Press
119 De Baets Street Winnipeg, MB R2J 3R9
www.wordalivepress.ca

WORD ALIVE
—**P R E S S**—

Cataloguing in Publication information can be obtained from Library and Archives Canada.

I joyfully transmit (dedicate) this variant (book) to my chary wife, Nida, my wary daughter, Di, and my witty son, Christian.

Also, I regard this book as a mental vaccine for my dear readers. If the pandemic robbed you of fun, read it as a booster shot to revitalize your zest in life, post-pandemic.

Acknowledgements

THE ENCOURAGEMENT AND support of my wife (Nida) and children (Christian and Di) afforded me the time to work on this manuscript. Their insight, experiences, and input sharpened the best punchlines and delivery of most of the stories. I loved it.

Social media made it possible for all my siblings to connect and interact. Bits and pieces of their funny stories found a resting place in this book. I would guess over 50.07 per cent of my siblings are funny folks too.

Scott, my workmate for over fifteen years, contributed his interesting, honest, true-to-goodness, and authentic life experiences, adding "msg" to so many funny moments of our everyday work routines. Almost every morning there was something he wanted to share. We were able to twist a sad story into something funny.

Les, the courier guy, almost every day brought a smile and raw, unfiltered, sometimes fake news about world events and COVID. His yapping and blabbing carried grains of truth and insights wrapped in funny stories. For him, the pandemic was a joke. There were always variants stories coming out. He even questioned which story was believable—the ones coming from the government or from the radio talk shows. And he was happy to share the same with us. Once he was out of the office, our confusion about the pandemic was compounded.

Bob was our office cleaner. Within an hour after Les exited the door, Bob's greetings altered our serenity. A bottle of a disinfectant in one hand and a cloth in the other made perfect his storytelling. The rhythm of wiping the table and relating his funny stories seemed calibrated and synchronized to perfection.

My small group in the community and the Diaryo Alberta Society both added funny and insightful experiences during the pandemic. Our close, dynamic, and trusting relationship exposed us to so many stories of people that added lots of pleasant memories.

Finally, I thank the Author of Life and His written Word that records the water turning to blood, frogs, lice, flies, livestock pestilence, boils, hail, locusts, darkness, and the killing of firstborn children—all of which were, more or less, comparable to the COVID-19 pandemic. God allowed these plagues to give people a lesson in life. Funny, the Israelites' survival was made possible not because of the kind of mask they wore, or by keeping the prescribed distance from each other, or isolating, or taking a certain brand of vaccine.

Foreword

IN *FUNDEMIC MOMENTS*, the author fearlessly invites us into his world, sharing a collection of funny, thoughtful, and insightful observations from his own unique perspective during the pandemic. This book isn't just a collection of comedic anecdotes but a heartfelt reminder of the power of laughter and storytelling to bring us together during challenging times.

The author's intention to provoke thought and understanding through humour is evident on every page. With wit and charm, he guides us through a journey of relatable experiences, touching on events, news, people, public health mandates, and the overall rollercoaster of life during the pandemic. His ability to find the funny side of even the most sombre moments is truly remarkable.

What sets *Fundemic Moments* apart is its purposeful celebration of the human spirit. The author encourages us to share our own funny stories, recognizing that laughter has the incredible ability to bring joy and create lasting memories. By sharing his own *Fundemic Moments*, he inspires us to reflect on our experiences and find humour in the midst of adversity.

This book is a treasure trove of stories that future generations will cherish, chuckle at, and learn from. The author beautifully captures the essence of this extraordinary time, reminding us that even in the face of sadness, there is always room for laughter, connection, and growth. We're reminded of the resilience and strength of the human spirit. *Fundemic Moments* is a must-read for anyone seeking a lighthearted yet thought-provoking escape.

Prepare to be captivated by the author's infectious humour and insightful perspectives. As you turn the pages, you'll find yourself laughing out loud, pondering the deeper meaning behind the anecdotes, and perhaps even discovering your own fundemic moments along the way. So grab a copy today and allow yourself to be immersed in a world of laughter, reflection, and shared experiences. Embrace the power of *Fundemic Moments* and create lasting memories that will bring joy for years to come.

AnnaLiza Sta. Ana, Ph.D.
President, Aquinas College Inc., Calgary, Alberta

Preface

IT'S A HOAX! And so—I isolate, wash hands, wear mask, keep distance, limit contact with other people, wait for the vaccine and booster shots, and laugh until I remember that it isn't!

The worldwide distractions and health impacts of the pandemic were immense and will be felt for generations. The spread of the virus was swift, and millions of lives perished. Communities were on edge. Relationships were altered. There was so much grief and despair. The general mood was bleak, and it seemed no good would come out of this pandemic. Collectively, we felt that what was ahead was perilous. The common thread and theme of stories were gloom and doom.

On a personal level, though, there were stories and experiences seldom told or shared. Categorically, these stories were sad, insightful, reflective, concerning, and compelling. One aspect of the pandemic experience seemed to be less written and journaled about, highlighted, and shared with others—the lighter, inspiring, uplifting, and insightful personal stories and experiences.

My last book, *COVID-19 Fundemic*, published in 2020, delved mostly into the funny and lighthearted aspect of the pandemic, expressed through illustrations, drawings, poems, and musings. The purpose was to encourage and inspire readers to journal their funny experiences and stories.

The goal of this book, *Fundemic Moments*, is to share my funny, thoughtful, and insightful observations, experiences, and perspectives on events, news, people, public health mandates, and life in general during the pandemic. My intention is to stir and provoke readers to ponder and understand the importance of sharing and telling a funny story. In so doing, we can all look back and reminisce. The pandemic had its witty and funny side too. It won't only be seen as one of the saddest moments of our lives. There will always be fundemic moments in our lives that the next generation will cherish, chuckle at, and learn from.

Three years after, I came to believe that possibly my wife, son and daughter were close to the truth. In the workplace and at home, I was a nonessential worker!

Do you have funny stories and experiences during the pandemic? Give me a call. Let's chat and share our "Fundemic Moments."

Glossary

Source: Glossary for the COVID-19 Pandemic.
Translation Bureau, Government of Canada

THE PANDEMIC HAS created a plethora of terminologies. Scientists, public health officials, academic circles, and the government have arrived at various definitions, applications, and easy-to-understand examples. However, there is a way to wittily express the concepts in layman's terms. (*Italics indicate my experiential definitions.*)

Ageusia. The complete or partial loss of the sense of taste.

Every time I modify and improve a version of a dish, since the onset of the pandemic, my wife's ageusia intensified.

Airborne transmission. Airborne transmission occurs when infectious agents are transmitted through droplet nuclei, aerosols, and dust particles that travel more than one metre. Not to be confused with droplet transmission.

A friend of mine confided that one of the pandemic positives was masking. Airborne transmission of droplet nuclei, aerosols, and dust particles from her teen's yelling, whining, and swearing were minimized.

Animal-to-human transmission.

When my friend let Buster, his dog, lick his face.

Anosmia. The complete or partial loss of the sense of smell.

Even before the pandemic, our office had a "no scent policy."

Antibody. A protein produced in response to the introduction of an antigen in an organism and that plays a role in the immune response against this antigen.

It's just like sweat produced by the body to cool it off from and internal and external stimulant. When my bank account statement losses two digits, my antibodies are looking for an antigen.

Antigen. A substance that, when introduced into an organism, induces an immune response.

I had it every morning. Oatmeal immunizes me from hunger and cholesterol buildup.

Antipyretic Therapy. A treatment to reduce fever.

Antipyretic therapy is no match for fever-producing high bills and gas price increases.

Anti-vaxxer. A person who is opposed to vaccination.

My older sister always reminded us to follow all public-health-mandated measures during the pandemic. However, she has not been vaccinated since the start of the pandemic.

Anti Viral Drug. A drug that works against a virus.

Of course!

Asymptomatic. Not exhibiting any symptoms.

My wife and I were asymptomatic, and we didn't even know it!

Booster Dose. A dose of an immunizing agent that reinforces or restores the immunizing effect of the original dose.

Looks like my friend's car—it has a booster installed. It travels faster and riskier, I guess!

Booster Shot. The injection of a dose of an immunizing agent that reinforces or restores the immunizing effect of the original dose.

It's just to boost the claim (and swell the bottom line) of the vaccine makers. Just saying.

Booster Vaccine. A vaccine that reinforces or restores the immunizing effect of the first vaccine administered against a given disease or infectious agent.

Meaning the first vaccine was not really that effective. Right?

Border Closure.

When my wife wasn't feeling well and not in the mood to look at my face during the lockdown, border closure in the house was reinforced!

Bubble. A bubble is formed by people, not necessarily from the same household, who agree to create a group in which physical distancing measures aren't mandatory. The number of people allowed in a bubble can vary from one place to another. However, a bubble is a closed group—that is, once the bubble is formed, its members can't change, and they can't be part of another bubble.

Freedom Convoy protest or the Canadian parliament during the pandemic?

Canada COVID-19. A mobile application that allows users to receive the latest updates on COVID-19, access trusted resources, and assess their symptoms.

I consulted Google. Presto, I got all the pandemic info I could possibly want to know, 24/7. The question is: How reliable is the info source?

Canada Emergency Response Benefit. The program that replaced the Emergency Care Benefit and the Emergency Support Benefit.

Pundits say this is one of the triggers to long-term economic collapse, called "Econdemic."

CE Business Account.

Are there still business accounts to account?

CE Commercial Rent Assistance.

I heard that one entrepreneur took the money and used it to close his business.

CE Rent Subsidy.
Or else more homeless in the streets and/or more landlords smiling.

CE Response Benefit.
More CPR! Victims are non-responsive.

CE Student Benefit.
From mom-and-pop residency plus this one—cool millennials!

CE Wage Subsidy.
For all CEOs receiving millions?

Canada Recovery Benefit.
Let's hope this one is a recoverable benefit.

Canada Recovery Caregiving Benefit.
Just give them the benefit of the doubt.

Canada Recovery Sickness Benefit.
The best benefit is to recover from sickness.

Circuit Breaker Lockdown. A relatively short lockdown with a set end date.
When my wife shut down, restricted, and curfewed me at home temporarily.

Communicable Period. The period during which an infectious agent may pass directly or indirectly from an infected person to another person.
The period during which a fake news or posting passes directly or indirectly from a gullible person to another gullible person, like me.

Community Spread/Transmission. The transmission of an infectious disease among a group of people that is not linked to contact with a person returning from a known area of infection or from contact with an infected person.
I was wondering if our Members of Parliament were included in this definition.

Comorbidity. In a person, the occurrence of one or more diseases, disorders, risk factors, or pathological processes at the same time as a given medical condition.

What a morbid reality.

Conjugate Vaccine. A vaccine in which two compounds have been combined to increase its effectiveness.

"Pfizerna?"

Contact Tracing. The process of finding people who may have been exposed to a person with an infectious disease to ensure that they are aware of the possible exposure and to follow up with them. Contact tracing involves three steps: contact identification, contact listing, and contact follow-up.

We have been subjected to this process for too long. If you have electronic gadgets and/or a social media account, then you can be traced or tracked. Right?

Convalescent Plasma. The antibody-rich plasma of someone who is recovering from an infectious disease. The body of a person with an infectious disease produces antibodies. These antibodies remain in the plasma to shield the person from reinfection. In theory, the antibodies could be used to treat other people with the same disease.

So now after three years of the pandemic, there are millions of people around the world from whom WHO can harvest this plasma for better use?

COVID-19 Symptom Self-Assessment Tool. A Government of Canada website that offers advice based on the answers given to symptom-self-assessment questions. It provides links to provincial and territorial assessment tools and information.

The question is: Which site is more reliable, this one or the others also found on Google?

COVID-19 Vaccine Global Access Facility. A global initiative aimed at working with vaccine manufacturers to provide all countries equitable access to safe and effective vaccines against COVID-19 once they are licensed and approved.

Is this the exclusive distributor and marketing arm of the pharma companies?

COVID-19 Virtual Assistant. An online tool that provides information on COVID-19.

There are hundreds of these tools. More tools on the way!

COVID Trends. An online tool that provides summary data on COVID-19 in Canada by health region.

Most common trends? New variants are coming out. More confusing health mandates, ineffective vaccine doses, and more booster shots are everywhere. These trends make me dizzier.

Curfew. A ban on being outside one's home between specific hours.

Mine is from 8:00 p.m. to 5:00 a.m.

Diagnostic Test. A laboratory analysis or method of examination used to confirm or rule out a diagnosis.

If you are positive—negative feeling. If you are negative—positive feeling.

Digital Tracking. The use of the geolocation feature on personal communication devices to monitor the movement of people in order to detect possible exposure to a disease or infectious agent.

Mobile phone providers and the government are doing this already.

Disinformation. The dissemination of deliberately false or misleading information with the intention of influencing the opinions of those who receive it.

Sometimes my wife and daughter tell me I am a carrier of fake news, plain and simple!

DNA Vaccine. After the DNA vaccine is administered, the DNA contained in the vaccine is transcribed into RNA in a cell without entering the nucleus. The RNA is then translated to produce antigens that will stimulate the immune response. Since the vaccine doesn't contain the whole virus, it doesn't cause infection.

Why not just call it a genetically modified vaccine?

Double Masking. Double masking involves layering one mask over another, generally a non-medical mask over a medical mask. This is usually done to help improve fit and filtration.

One time I tried it. One for the virus and the other one to minimize the build up of boogers.

Drive-through Screening Clinic. A facility at which people are screened for a specific disease without having to leave their vehicle.

While driving one late afternoon, I had a bout of polyphagia, also known as hyperphagia. The first fast-food drive-though screened and medicated my longing for food. Hunger gone, I went ahead to my next appointment.

Dyspnea. Difficulty breathing or a subjective feeling of breathing discomfort.

I had this one time when my card was maxed out and a close friend was infected with the virus.

Elbow Bump. The elbow bump is a way of greeting each other without shaking hands.

It worsens my tennis elbow.

Endemic. A disease that is constantly present or reappears at specific periods of the year.

If not for COVID, I would just think of national and local elections as normal occurrences.

Epidemic. The occurrence of a higher number of disease cases than expected in a given area over a specific period of time.

Driving during rush hour, merging onto Memorial Drive from downtown, the spot was epidemic with RRSD: "road rage syndrome disease."

Epidemiology. The study of the distribution and determinants of health-related states or events in specified populations.

There were never-ending talks about it in Canada: "Canuckiology"?

Extubation. The removal of a hollow tube that was inserted through the mouth or nose into the trachea to keep the airway open.

It was done once and even before the pandemic—the cancellation of the pipeline project.

Face Shield.

I tried it once, but my sight, smell, and smile protested. My wife too. She prefers to see my face when I'm wrong and she's right.

Flatten the Curve. Take measures to slow down the increase in the number of cases of an infectious disease to avoid overwhelming the health care system at the epidemic peak.

I started to lessen my carb consumption too!

Fomite. An object or a surface that can harbour an infectious agent and be a means of transmission.

Everything around and including me? Oh, no!

Gargle Lavage. Is a method used to collect a sample.

My wife uses chopsticks.

Genome Sequencing. This technique can detect all virus variants, even new variants.

My wife and daughter are good at detecting the sequence of my lying. Duh!

Hemoptysis. The coughing up of blood originating from the lower respiratory tract.

Oh. No! Call 911, fast!

Herd Immunity. The resistance of a group to the spread of an infectious disease based on the resistance to infection of a high proportion of individual members of the group.

Even before the pandemic, my wife and I desired to become members of a seniors' organization. The public health information categorized those at the age sixty and over as one of the most vulnerable groups to be infected with the virus. We looked at each other and agreed we could still hold off on this desire.

Host Cell. A cell invaded by an infectious agent.

My cell phone was invaded by an infectious hacker.

Hypercytokinemia. A disproportionate release of cytokines following over-stimulation of the immune system.

Why make it hard to pronounce?

Hypoxemia. A decrease of the oxygen content in arterial blood.

This happens whenever I have my bloodwork done. My pale skin says so.

Immune Response. The activity of the immune system that targets foreign substances.

It's not applicable to all the foreign substances that go to my tummy after a potluck with friends.

Immunogenic. That which can induce an immune response.

Just call it trigger!

Incubation Period. The period between the contamination of a susceptible host by an infectious agent and the onset of signs and symptoms of an infectious disease.

When you find out the food is expired, don't push your luck, or the bathroom will always welcome you with an open door.

Indirect Contact Transmission. This involves contact between a fomite and the person who becomes infected. This kind of transmission also occurs when a healthy person touches an infected person, doesn't wash their hands well, and then touches another person and infects them.

Monkeypox?

Infodemic. An excessive amount of information about a crisis, whether accurate or not, that is disseminated rapidly and uncontrollably.

We've all been in this for over three years now. Right?

Intubate. Insert a hollow tube through the mouth or nose into the trachea to keep the airway open.

It minimizes your spouse's rapid talking too.

Isolation. A preventative measure against the spread of an infectious disease that involves separating an infected person from non-infected people during the communicable period of the disease.

Those were the days, my friend. We thought would never end ....

Lung Infiltrate.

Smoking?

Mean Incubation Period. The mean is the value that each part of a sum would have if each part was equal.

That wasn't so mean at all!

Pandemic Modelling.

When there are no models catwalking on the stage because of public health measures like masking and distancing.

Molecular Test. Molecular tests detect the genetic material of a virus.

So what if we know the genetic material of the virus? What does it matter to peasants like us?

mRNA Vaccine. After the mRNA vaccine is administered, the body of the vaccinated person produces antigens by translating the administered mRNA. The antigens then stimulate the immune response. Since the vaccine doesn't contain the whole virus, it doesn't cause infection. Furthermore, the vaccine's mRNA doesn't enter the nucleus of the cell.

Oh, yeah? Of course, why not, sure, go for it. Whatever ...

Mutation. A change in the genetic material of an organism.

I was reminded of my daughter's toy—Ninja Turtle.

Mix and Match Vaccine.

It's like when you want the best of both Coke and Pepsi.

N95 Mask. Filters airborne particles and provides a very close facial fit.
Makes bad breath less obvious, covers stained teeth, and hides how many front teeth are missing.

Negative Pressure Room. A room in which the air pressure is lower than that of the adjacent rooms.
When my spouse tells my daughter to clean up her bedroom.

Non-Essential Worker.
My wife and daughter look at me at the same time.

Nosocomial Infection/Hospital-acquired Infection.
Not so comical infection when health care professionals are the sources of infection in a hospital.

Outbreak. An epidemic limited to a localized increase in the incidence of a disease.
The outbreak of lockdowns increased the number of online gamblers, bankruptcies, and drug addiction.

Oxygen Therapy. Also known as supplemental oxygen. The use of oxygen as a medical treatment.
Exactly what's needed when my wife's voice hits the roof because I purchased the wrong item from the grocery store.

Pandemic. An epidemic occurring worldwide or over a very wide area, crossing international borders and usually affecting many people.
In the form of poverty, food shortages, racism, cancel culture, political correctness, wokism, bigotry, socialism, extremism, elitism, culture wars, hate, etc.

Pandemic Fatigue. The loss of motivation to follow public health measures that emerges gradually over time and is influenced by the emotions, experiences, and perceptions of the person affected by a pandemic.
One weekend my wife asked if I would be preparing the same breakfast. I said yes. What's wrong with eggs, spam, and fried rice?

Pathogenicity. The capability of a pathogen to cause a disease.

During lockdown, my neighbour confessed that his in-laws and community bylaws were his worst pathogens.

Pay Disruption.

It also means bill payment disruption!

Personal Protective Equipment.

In the early days of the pandemic, a family doctor emailed and asked his office cleaner what PPE is. This is a true encounter, folks.

Person-to-person Transmission.

The very efficiency, effectiveness, and essence of gossip. My wife and I agree.

Physical Barrier.

Surgical mask, medical mask, face shield, and distance. Isn't it overkill!

Physical Distancing. A strategy to avoid the spread of an infectious disease in which crowded places, large gatherings, and close contacts are avoided and a distance determined by public health authorities is kept between people.

Early in 2022, there was a story of one city in Asia that physically restricted families and forced them to isolate. People were locked in, and the government rationed the needs of the people. Restricting mobility is worse than keeping distance.

Plank the Curve. Take rigorous measures to drastically slow down the increase in the number of cases of an infectious disease to avoid overwhelming the health care system at the epidemic peak.

Governments even resorted to a vaccine lotto. Even if this one was free, we didn't do it.

Plant-based Vaccine Production Technology. A technology that uses plants as bioreactors to produce virus-like particles.

How it is different from plant-based meat patties?

Portal of Entry. The anatomic site at which an infectious agent enters a host's body.

I wonder if my big mouth and flat nose fit the definition!

Portal of Exit. The means by which an infectious agent leaves a host's body.

Well, my wildest imagination is working.

Positivity Rate. The percentage of tests performed having a positive result.

I was reminded of a younger couple who bought a pregnancy test kit from a dollar store. At first the result was negative. Hours later, unconvinced, the husband picked the kit up from the garbage. It was positive.

Pre-symptomatic. Not yet exhibiting symptoms.

So what are the symptoms of pre-symptomatic, then? How do we know a person is pre-symptomatic?

Prevalence. The number of people in a population with a specific disease or condition at a given time, usually expressed as a proportion of the number of affected people to the total population.

The prevalence of people with anxiety, depression, and burnout is increasing. Sad.

Public Health Crisis.

When the government sides with one group over the other during the pandemic. One example is the vaccinations. If fully vaccinated people can be infected again, then what is this vaccination for? Public health crises arise when these groups meet at the rotunda and shame each other.

Quarantine. A measure to prevent the spread of an infectious disease in which a healthy person who may have been exposed to an infected person is isolated during the incubation period of the disease.

It's also a short period of time when a husband forgets his wife's birthday and their wedding anniversary. Isolation and incubation ensured.

Recombinant DNA Vaccine. A vaccine produced using genetic engineering techniques.

In short, this is a genetically modified vaccine.

Replicate. When a virus replicates, it uses a host cell's machinery to produce copies of itself.

Even a virus has the capacity to use a 3-D photocopier machine.

Respiratory Droplets. Respiratory droplets are relatively large and generally travel less than two metres after being expelled. They're produced by sneezing, coughing, breathing heavily, talking, and by some medical or dental procedures.

I wonder if respiratory droplets are present during the debates or Question Period in the House of Commons.

Respiratory Hygiene. Actions aimed at decreasing the dispersion of microorganisms expelled when sneezing, coughing, or blowing one's nose.

Why don't they just call it "cover your mouth, please. And shut up!"

Saliva-based Test. A test done on a saliva sample to detect an infectious agent.

What about the snout-based test? The infectious agent is also stuck in it, right?

Screening. The term "screening" is generally used to refer to the detection of a disease in asymptomatic people. However, in the context of the COVID-19 pandemic, the meaning of the term has been extended to include the administration of tests to detect infection in suspect cases.

But the question is: How do you know if the person in asymptomatic?

Serological Test. A test that detects the presence of antibodies against a specific infectious agent in a blood serum sample.

It's like a taste test that detects the presence of monosodium glutamate in a food.

Severe Acute Respiratory Syndrome Coronavirus 2. The virus that causes COVID-19.

Flu and cold viruses are its stooges.

Silent Hypoxia. A very low blood oxygen level that doesn't result in observable signs.

So how do you know a person has silent hypoxia if there are no observable signs?

Spike Protein. A transmembrane protein arranged in groups of three on the surface of the SARS-CoV-2 virus, which gives it its characteristic crown-like appearance.

Spike carbs appear when a person gains weight and a barrel-like appearance in the mid-body part.

Super Spreader. A single contagious person who contaminates a disproportionately large number of people compared to the number of people contaminated by the average contagious person.

The person is a close relative of a social media influencer, in person.

Swab. A stick with one end covered in an absorbent material that is used to collect a sample.

I use it every day in my ears after a shower.

Test Negative.

Positive news.

Test Positive.

Negative news.

Trace Contacts. Find people who may have been exposed to a person with an infectious disease to ensure that they're aware of the possible exposure and to follow up with them.

A close competitor of the FBI?

Triage. The assignment of degrees of urgency.

It's not located in Bermuda Triangle.

Vaccinated Person.

A person with a needle-poked arm once, twice, thrice, and possibly four times.

Vaccine Hesitancy. The delay in accepting or the refusal of a vaccine despite the availability of vaccination services.

The anti-vax lite group.

Vaccine Immunity. The protection against a disease or infectious agent provided by a vaccine.

Still in the process of validation after months of vaccinating millions of people around the world.

Vaccine Nationalism.

Charity begins at home. If in excess, share with your neighbours.

Vector. An insect or a living carrier that transports an infectious agent from an infected host to a susceptible host, their food, or their immediate surroundings.

Once the transfer is completed—they call it a victor!

Viremia. The presence of viruses in the blood.

Mama Mia. Hasta la vista.

Virulence. The measure of the severity of the disease caused by a specific infectious agent.

When a fake post went viral with over a million likes.

Virus-like Particle. A particle that can induce an immune response against a virus by mimicking its external structure but that can't cause infection, since it doesn't contain the viral genome.

Whatever!

Virus Variant. A virus that differs from the original virus strain because of mutations.

This virus variant is muted too.

Virus Variant of Concern.

Omicron to moronic?

Voluntary Quarantine. A measure to prevent the spread of an infectious disease in which a healthy person who may have been exposed to an infected person chooses to isolate themselves.

After a night of unsettled spousal conflict.

World Health Organization. The World Health Organization is the directing and coordinating authority for health within the United Nations system. It's responsible for providing leadership on global health matters, shaping the health research agenda, setting norms and standards, articulating evidence-based policy options, providing technical support to countries, and monitoring and assessing public health trends.

In simple terms—What? How? Oh no!

Zoonosis. An infectious disease that can be transmitted from animals to humans either directly, indirectly, or by a vector.

Hot dogs, hamburgers, fried chicken, BBQs, etc. Still in doubt?

Moments

AS THE PANDEMIC moved across the land, people's experiences and lives were impacted. The "norm" was altered. Along the way, however, not all encounters were unpleasant. Some deserve attention and serve as life-lessons. Others are witty, funny, and at best, hilarious. The following are just some of my unique observations and experiences.

IT'S A HOAX!
And so—I isolate, wash hands, wear a mask, keep my distance, limit contact with other people, wait for the vaccine and booster shots, and laugh until I remember that it isn't!

IN CASH
On the first Sunday after the pandemic was declared, the phone rang. "Yup," I replied to my sister on the other line. "We're not going to church today." However, I assured her that our Sunday spiritual practice was taken care of.

"How?" she inquired.

"Your niece will lead in praise and worship. I'll deliver the message, and your sister-in-law will collect the offering. As usual—she prefers cash!" No e-transfer!

NON-ESSENTIAL
During the second week into the pandemic, our office sent out a directive that only essential personnel were required to report in person. I told my officemate, "It's not good for me to stay home."

"Why?" he responded.

"It affirms my wife's observation."

"What's that?" he said.

"I'm a non-essential worker!"

DRY SPONGES

In the early weeks of isolation, children were like dry sponges. They absorbed all kinds of routines and information they encountered at home with their parents.

"Yup, including most of the items in the fridge," says one of my kids.

SWITCH SIDES

My wife and I have achy bodies. Her pain congregates on left side, mine on the right. COVID kept us two feet apart while sleeping. She slept on her left side, and I on my right. Every week thereafter, we switched sides!

BANK POLICY

Before the pandemic, you couldn't enter a bank while wearing a mask. Now you can't enter banks without a mask.

COMPETITION

Four rooms are competing for my attention and time during lockdown: kitchen, bed, living, and washroom.

AFFIRMATIVE

Most politicians use masks and distance effectively. Masking true intentions and distancing from promises. Affirmative.

THE FACTORS

Distance and time of exposure are two of the many ways to stop the spread of the virus. These are the same factors that weaken and deteriorate the bond of relationship.

STORE ACTIVITY

A conversation I overheard on the phone between my wife and her sister: Their friend Tony had been transferred to the only open coffee shop at a college campus in Calgary. The following day, despite pleas and protest by all staff, the store was shut down. Management didn't listen to their argument that customers were still coming.

The daily average was six customers—two in the morning, two at noon, and two before closing. The management showed them footage of a day's worth of activity in the store. Six different men in uniform for the whole day was not enough to keep the store open.

ALL NATURAL

Masks limit the spread of the virus. There is also a kind of mask people wear daily. They wash it in the morning. All natural and non-GMO. Over time it wrinkles. The mirror reflects it. Its purpose is to protect good impression and hide frustrations.

GOOD IDEA?

Weeks into the pandemic, one of the building maintenance guys visited our office and left us with his interesting tip on how he protected himself from the virus. Every time he went to an establishment to eat, shop, and stock up, he'd stop for a minute at the entrance. If he heard a cough or sneeze in the distance, that was his cue to leave.

Good idea, I thought.

The moment he opened the door to leave, he let out a loud cough.

NATURAL REMEDY

The isolation slowed down my physical activities, and the pain in my right knee intensified. Google led me and my wife to explore other pain-relief options available on the market.

One Saturday morning, we drove to Community Natural Food Market. Non-GMO and natural foods of all kinds on the shelving waved at us. Our objective was to find the black cherry magic juice, or whatever it was called. New to the place, we asked a saleslady. She asked, "Is that the one for gout?"

With a forced smile, I said, "Yes."

We beamed with excitement to be close to the counter where the black cherry was located.

Prior to coming to the store, I suggested we buy two bottles of this stuff. We grabbed just one bottle, the only available size.

On the way out, my limping worsened, and my pocket felt sore, as the bottle cost more than three BBQ chickens from Costco. Keeping healthy is indeed expensive.

Our consolation was to extend the use of this black cherry potion for as long as I could. So instead of a glass a day, we whipped out the tablespoon and diluted the juice with the always-available and forever-free water.

SORT OF SANITARY

The parking lot was full. Clearings along the banks of the river were occupied by people of all colours. Social distancing seemed to be in the distant past. Very few had their masks on. I was one of the few. Moments later, we reached the mouth of the Sheep River Falls, located in the belly of K-Country. Walk, talk, eat, and never-ending selfies occupied the time of isolation-weary folks. Time with nature and friends proved refreshing, relaxing, and calming.

Noticeable also was the line of people in front of the only restroom in the park. "Use at your own risk" was posted on the doors. Sanitizer and toilet paper gone. Nevertheless, just metres away from the crowd, two heads peeked out amongst thick bushes.

It was an aura of relief and nature's way of saying, "Come all you who are weary and heavy laden ..."

HAIL!

On the last day of August 2021, Calgary's weather was weird, as usual. Warnings of scattered thunderstorms in and around Calgary were issued, including for Strathmore.

My colleague, a part-time fireman in the town, shared his experience with us the following day. They'd been scheduled to refresh their water rescue training in one of the lakes in town. When they set out for the training, the hail hit hard.

"So your training was cancelled because of the thunderstorm?" I asked.

"Yup!" he answered.

I guess their rescue suits are designed only for underwater exposure.

PRESSURE

Our building operator notified us that a water contractor would check and assess the quality of our water. The source and the water lines would be tested too. "Are they going to adjust the water pressure too?" I asked my officemate.

"Nope!" he said.

The existing pressure was good enough for a car wash at the dock area back of the office. We both smiled.

BLINK, BLINK, BLINK, OPEN!

Over four months of waiting was a long time. Two weeks ago, after over an hour of sitting in the reception room, the receptionist had led me to the eye surgeon's office. The usual procedures took place. I left the clinic with my scheduled two more appointments before the actual removal of my cataract.

Weeks later, my first appointments were impressive. Five minutes before the assigned time, I was attended to. Cool!

My eyes went into five or six tests. One very small vial of eye drops, I guessed, went empty too. One thing I appreciated, though, was the standard mantra of the med assistants.

Once back home, I asked my wife if she could introduce to her workplace the new song I'd discovered and learned at the clinic.

"What was it?" she inquired.

I said, "Blink, blink, blink—open wide, open, open, open! Blink, blink, blink."

SUMMER OUTINGS

Our weekends during the summer of 2021 were occupied, health-wise. We trekked parks and mountain trails, averaging 5K. Results were amazing. Stamina increased and forelegs firmed up. Topics of talks along the trail were unlimited. Loud and fast conversation killed time and distance to the point of annoyance, sometimes.

One Friday my colleague asked, "Where will you drive this weekend?"

"Smash Head Buffalo Run and Old Man River Dam," I said with excitement. Curious, he inquired why we'd picked those places. "If the cliffs of the smash head buffalo run aren't deep enough, then we'll still have the freezing water of the dam for people who talk and gossip too loud, fast, and much," I said.

"Why haven't I thought that before?" he gleefully commented.

We both "lolled."

ART APPRECIATION

Glenbow Museum in Calgary was set to close for three years for upgrades and renovations. Two weeks before the closing, my wife, a friend, and I took advantage of the free pass.

The visit, our second time there, was not eventful. Paintings by prominent painters from around the world adorned the walls of the second storey. Animals, livestock, places, and people were depicted realistically.

Halfway into our roaming in and between halls, I noticed my wife. Her curiosity was intense as her eyes scanned the hanging photos in their entirety. Up, down, and sides. I strode leisurely and immersed myself in the beauty and awe of the exhibits.

I asked her, "Why do you stay so long at each photo exhibit?"

"I'm more interested in the design, material, and beauty of the photo frame," she said in all seriousness. She remembered my plan to frame few of my treasured shots. I got her point.

One of the hanging art works was of a group of animals. Superimposed on it was a walrus. I took a photo of it to show to my daughter. Anything with a walrus makes her chuckle. She would love it, I guessed.

Back home at dinner time, we shared our day's long experiences. I shared how my wife enjoyed the frames and how she preferred to check in on the different designs of the paintings' frames. With excitement, I picked up my phone and showed the photo to my daughter.

"Cool," she said. "What's the name of the artist?"

Oops ...

My wife's focus was on the frame. Mine was on the painting itself. My daughter's was on the artist.

Like the art of dealing with the COVID-19 pandemic. Mask, distance, and vaccine — these are the basics of understanding and coping with the pandemic.

HERO'S VARIANT

Occasionally we tended to get out from our isolation. A plan was made. We left Calgary one weekend and headed out on a two-hour drive to Radium. We enjoyed the place and the scenery. Days later, the drive home was boring.

Both sides of Highway 93 from Calgary to Radium were sprinkled with various scenic spots for travellers to enjoy. Creeks, ponds, cliffs, trails, waterfalls, and other spots compete for the attention of visitors and explorers. Selfies and real time FB postings were never-ending.

Interestingly, within a span of eighty-six kilometres on that highway, two waterfalls beg for attention: Tatakaw and Numa. Comparatively, Numa is just like a bust in size, while Tatakaw towers like a full-body scale monument. The same elements of beauty, though, are present: mountain backdrop, falling water, a flowing hum, and a cooling mist. Nature's workmanship and beauty are unparalleled. Perfectly spaced, visitors have all the reason to stop by for a quick selfie, snack, and bio break.

A parallel situation exists over a stretch from Calgary to Airdrie. Roughly twenty minutes, or the thirty-five-kilometre drive from Calgary to Airdrie, is just a warmup. No need for a restroom or stop over. For Filipino-Canadians visiting these two cities, two interesting new spots were in the making: a bust in Airdrie and a monument, in a year's time, in Calgary of the Philippines' national hero, Jose Rizal. A full-bodied monument was the coronavirus. The bust, oh well, was the variant.

"The monument or bust of a hero was inspiring. Erecting the same hero's memory thirty-five kilometres apart was ridiculous." The COVID-19 virus was the monument. The Omicron variant was the bust. Just saying! (As of this writing the planned monument was not built).

WORST LEADERS?

Weeks into the pandemic, Bob came to our office every day to sanitize tables, counters, doorknobs, light switches, etc.

One Monday morning, he confirmed if I was from the Philippines. I said yes, with pride! Then he informed me that Digoy (former Philippine president Rodrigo Duterte) was one of the worst world leaders. I inquired which fake news outlet that info came from. He'd watched it on YouTube the night before. No wonder.

Sad, but he said, "Just saying."

MASKING

The opening of the province from the grip of the pandemic was welcome news. However, the habit of being cautious—wearing masks and distancing—was still entrenched deeply into most of the population. In public places, most people were still unrecognizable and keeping themselves separated by two metres.

"If you have the second shot and are feeling healthy, you don't need the mask or to distance," said my friend. He'd just gotten back from Costco. "Still, many people are crazy with their mask on," he whined aloud.

"Or they saw you coming, so they put on their mask and distanced themselves from you." We both laughed. Then he walked out the door, coughing.

"No wonder people use their mask." Just saying.

BOTTOM LINE

The 2021 Stampede breakfasts sure were magnets for politicians. More than a dozen of these events swarmed the city. The "Almusal," the one along 17th Avenue in the southeast, generously hosted by Pacific Hut Restaurant, various businesses, and community groups, was a blast. Even the heavens poured tears of joy that day. It didn't dampen the thirst, hunger, joy, and appreciation of the people.

The afternoon one held at Seafood City was equally impressive.

Interestingly and possibly, it was the most opportune day for politicians and leaders to show their care, concern, and blah blah blah to the community. Bottom line? They just needed people's votes and approval.

Rain or shine, masked or not, distanced or not—when an event offers free food, guess what—Pinoys' attendance was ensured, and politicians roared like lions.

BREATHE IN, HOLD IT, BREATHE OUT ...

In mid-September 2021, I had my doctor's appointment. He wanted to make sure my left lower ribs area was ok. Days later, I walked into the lab and was told to wait at least forty-five minutes. To make the most of my time, I proceeded to Shopper's Drug Mart in Chinook Mall, blocks away from the lab, to order my other prescribed medication.

The pharmacist looked at the prescription and said, "It may take about half an hour for this."

"No hurry," I said. I stepped out of the store and headed straight to Indigo bookstore. The computer wasn't working, so I had to ask one of the saleswomen where to grab *American Marxism* by Mark Levin. After a few minutes of looking around at the history and politics sections, she handed me the book. I grabbed another book by Daniel Silva.

The lady behind the till tried three times to process my payment via debit card. It wasn't only their computer book catalogue not working. I agreed to her suggestion that she hold the book for me to pick up later that day. I had no choice. I looked at the time and saw that I only had ten minutes to walk from the bookstore to the parking lot and eventually to the lab.

With a smile, the receptionist remembered my appointment. After a few minutes of waiting, I was ushered into the changing room and was told to wait for my turn. I was called after five people and forty minutes of waiting.

I observed as the technician prepped my position. She spoke this mantra: "Breathe in, hold it, and breathe out." Six positions and her mantra uttered at the same tone, frequency, and tune.

Before I proceeded out the door, I told her, "I learned one thing today."

"What was that?" she inquired.

Different labs have their own mantras. My optical check mantra is "blink, blink, and blink, open." The mantra of my dentist is "Open, open, and open more." "Relax, relax, and take a deep breath," was the mantra of the med tech taking my blood. In the imaging lab, it's "Breathe in, hold it, breath out."

The COVID pandemic has created a mantra too: MDV, or mask, distance, and vaccine.

A JAB OR ONE'S JOB

"What's up?" I answered the call from an old friend.

"Nothing. Just want to touch base with you guys," she answered.

Minutes into our conversation, she indicated her frustration with her employer. Not only did the pandemic jeopardize her health, but now her job was on the line.

"Why?" I asked with my usual inquisitiveness.

They'd been mandated to take a jab on or before the end of the month, but she wasn't convinced the vaccine was best for her body.

"So what's the trade off?" I listened to her frustration and helplessness for another thirty minutes.

"A jab or no job is cruel," she said.

The risk of catching the virus and losing your job was a double whammy.

TRIBALISM

Amid the pandemic, and after a few weeks of intense electioneering, Canadians were back to where they'd been before. More of the same political and governance stuff plus over $600 million of the people's money wasted. The goal of getting a majority went kaput. The chance of forming a majority rule was slim for the coming generations of Canadians.

The statement "diversity is our strength" is a classic example of an oxymoron. There are now at least six political parties in Canada: Liberal, Conservative, NDP, Bloc, Green, and the People's Party. The greater the number of parties sprouting up based on their respective (diversified) ideological beliefs, the less Canadians come up with a solid consensus.

Everything boils down to the inherent instinct of humanity: tribalism.

ELECTION 2021

The over $600 million spent on the election of members of the House of Commons to the forty-fourth Canadian Parliament resulted in the status quo. It was more of the same.

A pandemically wasteful exercise.

VAXX ET AL
Vaxxed
Unvaxxed
Vaxx hesitancy
Anti-vaxx
Vaxx passport
Vaxx fest
Vaxx lotto
Vaxx booster
Vaxx choice
Vaxx exemption
Vaxx injury

CHOICES
Jab or job
Mask or half-mast
Covidiot or covid-smart
Booster shots or booster juice

PACMAN RETIRING!

The Philippines' $enator Money Pacquiao retired from boxing. His next goal was the seat of the President of the Philippines. He campaigned during the pandemic and never let up. Millions of pesos rained down the archipelago, and the pandemic became a secondary issue. People loved it. Money or manna from heaven. Why not?

A Pac-demic of Philippine politics.

DUAL CITIZEN

This past summer, my family and close friends and I spent our weekends hiking on various park trails in and around the province. On the first weekend of October 2021, by virtue of my age (I suppose), the group asked what time we would depart from a friend's place. We were heading to Banff's cave and basin site. A seven-thirty meeting and an eight o'clock departure were agreed upon.

For whatever reason, we were late arriving at the meeting place in Calgary. Ironically, the place was just a thirty-second—yes, thirty-second-drive—from our place. Soon we hit the road, and just over an hour later, we were just a few kilometres from our destination.

The phone rang. "We'll be there in three minutes," I said as I answered the call.

I absorbed their jokes and sarcasm as we gathered at the picnic bench for our lunch. I was spared from further humiliation by one of the moms in the group, who said, "As a dual citizen, Romy opted to follow his Filipino time." Lol.

RUNNING LATE

Five weeks before the local election in Calgary, I had a meeting with two community leaders. They confided to me the alleged wrongdoings of another leader. Corruption and malversation of funds were the obvious sins committed.

More issues cropped up. One candidate's run for the mayoral office was discussed. Someone from the Filipino community was one of the candidates. I shared my thoughts about it: "The courage to run is commendable, but the chance to win is slim." I presumed that running for this office was more of an effort at profile (personal and business) building. The exposure alone was money well spent. ROI at its best.

"Running for another position, like school trustee, is more promising than local politics," I added.

Our long meeting ended with delicious snacks.

Three weeks later, I received a phone call from one the guys I'd met. The other guy had put his name in the hat for the board of trustees in the separate school system on the very last day of registration. I enthusiastically welcomed the idea and even advised them to mobilize our respective networks of contacts.

Hours later, it dawned on me the conversation we'd had weeks before. The guy was running for office at the school board level. Whatever his reason, it was inspiring that one from the community was running. However, I had reservations as to why he'd submitted his candidacy on the last day of the registration. Others had registered months before the deadline.

Later, during the kickoff campaign, he explained that he was running due to pressure from friends. At the back of his campaign office was a big sign promoting his newly-opened business. Just saying.

NOBEL PEACE PRIZE 2021

Maria Ressa and Dmitry Muratov won the Nobel Peace prize in 2021 for their courageous fight for freedom of the press and expression.

Maria Ressa relentlessly exposes abuse of power, violence, and authoritarianism in the Philippines. The dirty deeds of President Duterte were ripe for reporting.

For several decades, Dmitry Muratov defended freedom of speech in his country amid challenging conditions and while bearing the pressure of Russia's president.

How would these two laureates address the plight of the persecuted unvaxxed population?

BISEXUAL SUPERMAN?

When the issue of the unvaxxed sector of our society was getting complicated, Bisexual Superman stirred the imaginations of many. I called it the "suffering man." What was super about this comic man anyway? He was just a comic character, a man manipulated by a culture clash and void of substance in terms of fighting COVID-19. Right?

SUPPLY CHAIN CRISIS
The result of the supply chain crisis was empty store shelves in major grocery stores across America. One store affected was a Christian bookstore. Demand for New International Version (NIV) Bibles was high, and inventories were low. The owner asked patrons to pray for the end of the supply chain crisis. One person asked why the NIV was singled out, and it was because the ink comes from Germany, the paper from Italy, the cover from France, and the glue from India. These supplies are shipped by various carriers. Printed in America

New International Version indeed.

ALBERTA ELECTIONS
In late 2021, Calgary elected the first female mayor of colour. Edmonton elected the first racialized mayor. The province opted to remove the equalization clause in the constitution and to fix daylight savings time. Amid the pandemic, everything was possible under the sun, if everyone followed the public health mandates.

PASSWORD
My daughter was good at organizing her stuff at home and in the workplace. Early in 2021, she made a secure file for all our electronic codes and passwords. It took her hours to access and organize the same. The task stressed her.

After less than an hour of napping, she got back to finalize the job. Stress came back coupled with confusion, and she forgot the password of the file where she'd stored our passwords.

The piece of paper she threw into the garbage full of used masks saved her day—and our password.

TO DO LIST
It was in late January 2021 when I got off early from work one day. I needed to meet the furnace guy, who would check my furnace and

clean the exhausts. Along the way, my daughter called. "Dad, can you take a picture of the paper on top of my computer in my room?" She'd forgotten to grab it and take it to her work. The paper was a "to do list for the day."

I sent her the photo with the text, "Put as # 1 on your list—don't forget the to do list!"

SAYINGS
"Boredom is one of the unwanted children of Pandemic Lockdown."

"Availability of the vaccine is good news. The ability to laugh is better news."

GLUE
One late afternoon, my workmate was busy working at the back of our office bay. Moments later, he screamed and asked me for help. He had accidentally squirted Crazy Glue into his right eye. He ran straight to our First Aid box, and with no time to spare, he pulled hard on the cover cap of the plastic eyewash solution. He poured out half the bottle into his eye.

The nurse at the other end of the line affirmed that his action was the right one.

Minutes after the incident, his composure returned to normal. Then I said, "We now have a problem."

"What?" he asked.

"We need to glue the broken plastic cap/cover of the eyewash."

"Nope," he said. "I'm not touching that glue again."

ISOLATE THE NEIGHBOURHOOD
Three mornings in a row, my workmate reported to work groggy. Late night and early morning emergency calls had kept them (volunteer firemen) busy. Less than a fifty-metre radius from his house, people, animals, and structural concerns were attended to with patience and professionalism.

The isolation made people too cautious. Small concerns sometimes called for emergency help.

He intoned, "We're exploring ways to minimize these kinds of incidents."

I responded, "Why don't you isolate your neighbourhood to the max?"

TRAVEL AROUND

My mate's wife was mad. Her plan to bring their frying pan to her office did not materialize. The pan had been brought into our office months ago. I inquired, "Looks like your frying pan has a passport to let it travel around from your place to our office and then to your wife's workplace."

He chuckled. "Just wait for our dishwasher."

Correct!

ALARM

In March, we received our new, individually-assigned office cell phone. Looked fancy, indeed. The gadget was, of course, for official use only. I asked my officemate, "What's the best use of this phone then? We still have our office landline number."

He responded, "Set it up as an alarm during our coffee break (nap) time in the office. It's official, right?"

LEVEL OF AUTHORITY

Our main responsibility was to inspect and assign grade to twenty-one Canadian grains. Technically, our service centre's operational undertakings—like paying bills, security, staffing—were handled by our regional office in Vancouver and/or our head office in Winnipeg. Anything related to financial and service transactions was above our pay grade.

One day a request for service was sent to us by the British Columbia government. Like a ping pong game, the matter was referred to us once again from the higher-ups in Vancouver.

"This is crazy!" said I.

My officemate responded, "What do they think of us? We're in a position to deal with this kind of transaction? Even at home we're not the ones deciding major decisions. Right?"

We both went lol.

JOKE BIDEN /TRUE DOUGH

Les, a courier guy, not only delivers mail and packages, but he always has something to blabber about.

"The US of America and Canada are transforming into authoritarian countries," he said one day. "The Chinese, Russians, Iranians, and North Koreans are having a field day because of the way the president and prime minister of the two countries govern. What a joke."

"Yup," I added. "That's why I heard that their president's name has changed to Joke Biden! And our Prime Minister? True Dough."

SONAR TECHNICIAN

Technically, a sonar technician is responsible for underwater surveillance. Mat, one of the youngest trainees in his class, explained his job in Halifax with the Canadian Navy.

They intercept and interpret information from all ocean vessels and ships passing in and out of the Canadian waters off Nova Scotia. "It's very interesting, Uncle," he said with pride.

I responded with glee. "So you now know how to intercept and interpret military gossip?"

"Oh, shoot!" he sighed.

STAND-UP COMEDIAN

A friend invited us to her sixtieth birthday on January 15, 2022. We arrived at the venue early, so about 80 per cent of the seating capacity was empty. Guests trickled in, and moments later the celebrant's entourage marched in, straight to the head table.

In no time, the room was filled with people beaming with joy and hunger, I guessed. Dressed up and well suited, everybody was in a pleasant mood.

The host calmed down the crowd, and everyone settled in. Instructions were stipulated. Each table had their time to take a photo shot with the celebrant and then proceeded to the food table. The process went smoothly.

The program began with much anticipation from the guests. The guest performer was introduced enthusiastically, and people gasped when they heard his name. He was one of the most popular stand-up comedians in the Philippines. Well fed and happy, the crowd greeted him with joy.

I looked at the tables the White guests were occupying. All the faces were crafted with great anticipation. Quite possibly it was their first time hearing a Filipino stand-up comedian deliver punchlines of wit and humour. I was also eager to hear his pieces and delivery. I love comedy too.

The comedian just sang for the celebrant—two songs that were possibly unknown to most of the guests.

We left the event with three observations. One, halfway through the program, over 75 per cent of the crowd willfully ignored the masking and distancing protocol. Two, the celebrant was overjoyed with the presence of her dear friends and former employer. Finally, I expected the comedian to deliver material that would make the gathering more fun and memorable to the celebrant and the guests as well.

The introduction and singing performance of the comedian were simply a joke.

LIKE MOTHER, LIKE DAUGHTER

His cell phone rang. No surprises there. The time of the call, manner of greetings, and topics being discussed seemed normal for a call from his wife. Moments into the call, my friend's tone of voice changed. Irritation was evident. His capitulation was obvious. His frustration was spoken out after their conversation.

"So you forgot again your wife's instructions?" I chuckled.

"Nope," he answered. "It was my daughter."

"Sorry, I thought it was your wife."

"Yeah, there's no difference between my wife and daughter."

I kept silent for ten minutes in my comfortable chair.

SNAKE

It was mid-August when our small group visited the Buffalo Head Smash Run Museum in southern Alberta. The entrance fee was not part of the plan. We just walked around the cliff on the east side of the facility. Both sides of the narrow path leading up the hill were surrounded by thick shrubs and small trees. The shade made our ascent easier. Leading the pack and metres ahead of me, a metre-long, slender, brownish snake crossed the path to the other side. It was the first time I'd seen a live one in years, and I was taken aback.

"Snake!" I shouted, loud enough to caution the rest of my friends behind me. We all stopped, listened, and looked around. Our anxiety went up.

Minutes passed, and composure and calmness got into us again. We resumed our walk at a faster pace. From behind came another scary shout: "Snake!" This time it was my very nervous wife.

I tried to extract a lesson and insight from this encounter. Until now, I haven't.

I guess it's all just coincidence. If you think of one lesson or insight, please don't hesitated to contact me.

Well, I guess that moment of fearing the unseen (virus) was an example of anxiety, and seeing the real danger was the real thing to be worried about.

PURPLE SWEATERS

For many years, Tim and Mel (not their real names) seemed to be avoiding each other for a reason known only to them. One night we met and had no choice but to congregate in one spot in the park. The ladies acted with civility, good faith, and a kind demeanour toward each other. Frozen relations thawed, and both ladies started to chat casually. At the end of the fireworks festival show, both were cordially exchanging jokes and even snacks.

Thanks to COVID and Global Fest 2021, the rift healed. What was interesting was that they both were wearing the same colour of sweater: purple. For peace.

BETTER BUY

My friend's wife was demanding. She wanted a new pair of shoes for their holiday trip to get away from isolation, so I tried to appease his gloomy morning: "Don't worry, your wife only needed a new pair of shoes. My wife's demand was a new shoe rack!"

WALMART TO THE RESCUE

As the host, unwinding from a stressful and fun-packed senior wedding ceremony of my friend Tony was the most needed break that one chilly February night. In one of the hotel rooms with some of the entourage members, we talked about and evaluated the ceremony and reception.

The bride's son shared his unforgettable experience. Hours before the start of the reception, he realized that he'd forgotten to bring the pants that went with his suit. His wife admonished him to double check his stuff next time. To drive home and back to the hotel would take him and hour and a half. Staring out the window in his only available pants, blue jeans, he saw that Walmart was only blocks away.

The remaining forty-five minutes proved helpful. With his wife and kid, they entered the room perfectly ok. The pants he bought from Walmart fit and were a perfect match to his suit.

We all agreed that the venue of the reception was perfect. Not even masking or distancing were observed.

Walmart, the saving grace for many, like Aydin.

THE WAY BACK

It was mid-afternoon on the last Saturday before Christmas when my wife, friend, and I drove to Chinook Mall. The traffic was heavy, so we decided to park under the mall's parking lot. The huge lot was full, so I pictured in my mind the orientation and spot where we parked the car. Confidently, we followed the sign leading to the exit stairs. Out we went in front of the Shopper's Drug Mart. We had to cross the narrow street alley to get into the mall.

Moments later, we ended up at our destination. The Fossil watch store was half-full of customers. The wristwatch given to us needed adjustments, so we waited for few minutes before we were attended to.

As we were just about to exit the store, this guy—fully PPEd—started talking to us. He was a Filipino who looked Korean. The greetings turned into a thirty-minute talk, mostly about him. He'd been married thrice and in a few months was getting married to his fourth. Photos of his house in the Philippines, his loving mother, and excelling daughter were proudly flashed before us.

As a freelance marketing consultant of two private schools in Calgary, he could afford to spend his time wisely and buy unbudgeted stuff like the watch he'd purchased from Fossil.

He asked us where we worked and if we were happy there. We sensed what he wanted us to know. He was better off than the rest of his fellow Filipinos, who were toiling hard just to maintain the lifestyle they wanted to keep. For him, the freedom he enjoyed was a way better life, he supposed. No house mortgage because he was just renting. No car to maintain, and no insurance and gas to pay. Public transit suited his mobility needs. No constraints with time or work quotas.

At first, we thought his arguments were reasonable. We just listened and nodded. Finally, our encounter with the guy ended with relief. We saw him outside waiting for the next bus to arrive. It was minus fifteen, and his shivering was obvious.

We went back in a hurry to the parking lot. The snowfall was getting heavy, and we needed to head home and beat the traffic. We took the elevator inside the mall going into the parking lot.

We then spent twenty-five minutes figuring out where the car was parked. The picture in my mind had been dimmed by the encounter with the guy, and I was bit disoriented. Patience thinned out. Our consensus was to trace back our steps. We emerged from the front door of Shoppers Drug Mart and crossed the alley. We then went through the stairway door and down into the parking lot. Presto! Less than a minute later, we found the car waiting for us in a corner.

Along Macleod Trail waiting for the traffic to move, I saw the bus coming from the Chinook Train Station and heading to the area where the guy was waiting and quivering.

It was different strokes for different folks.

RETIREMENT PLANNING

It took us months to get a spot for a retirement seminar. My workmate was turning fifty-five in May 2022, and I was thinking of retiring the last day of September of the same year.

Days before the event, course materials and assignments were emailed to us.

Nine other individuals had registered for this online course. We all worked for the federal government.

We made sure all our gadgets were working well and our background office looked like a typical government dig. We even talk about the best attire for the occasion.

I'd arrived an hour earlier for the final prep. Same with my mate. Minutes before the session started, we put on our best look—background, demeanour, and professionalism.

Mike, the facilitator, introduced himself. We waited but weren't told to introduce ourselves. Efficient as Mike was, his final housekeeping reminders were to keep our mics muted and that there was no need for him to see our faces during the session.

Background, demeanour, and good-looking attire went out the window. One good thing, though, was that we were able to take short naps in between topics.

SHOW OR SHOW OFF?

My officemate and his daughter (plus her boyfriend) went weekend skiing in Sunshine, and it went well except for a small bump. In his nth roll, he told the young ones how to handle the bump. Off he went, and for whatever reason, he flipped and landed with his head banging on the snow.

Daughter and boyfriend were worried. They hurried to assess my mate's situation. "His eyes are moving. He'll be okay," said the boyfriend. As a skateboarding instructor, he knew my officemate would be fine.

"So your idea of showing them how to conquer a bump in skiing turned into a bad show off?" I asked. We both laughed loud.

"Yeah, I guess so," he said.

RANDOM NEWS
My first dose of workplace intellectual nourishment came from comics and funny cartoons on mainstream online media. However, when the pandemic engulfed the world, my focus turned to COVID-19 related news updates, information, trends, and all the trimmings of absurdity, incompetencies, and inconsistencies of many government officials.

PERFECT EQUATION!
Omicron = Moronic

EXISTENTIAL THREAT?
Climate Change, Cancel Culture, Conversion therapy, CRT, COVID, China?

MANDATES
They disrupt the lives of both vaccinated and unvaccinated. Government's COVID mandates rip apart even the closest of family members and the economy. Why allow COVID to wreck the very fabric of our society?

FREEDOM BEGETS WISDOM
Curtailing freedom suffocates wisdom. Let wisdom freely flow. It will outperform COVID's pandemic show.

VARIANTS
COVID variants are alpha, beta, delta, omicron, etc.

Vaccine variants are four to twelve years old, twelve to seventeen years old, fifty to seventy years old, etc.

I wonder if this is all about the best and most profitable pharma business model of all time.

MY CREW
For over twenty years, my wife and I spent two hours max each weekday cleaning a doctor's clinic. A daily dose of physical exercise at its best in

a strip mall metres away from Gold's Gym. We walked out sweating the same as those who walked out of the gym.

One day the doctor texted me. His schedule was tight, and he had no time to clean his house, located on acreage in Heritage Point in the southeast corner of Calgary. He was looking for trustworthy people to do the job, and he pleaded for my wife and I to spare three hours to do the job one weekend. Extra exercise time and funds for shopping at the Cross Iron, we thought.

I texted him back: "My crew will be there around 2:00 p.m."

He replied, "Who are they?"

"My 'wifi' and daughter."

"Funny one," came his reply.

PRE-RETIREMENT CHIT CHAT

One week after attending a two-day pre-retirement seminar, I planned to share the info, insights, and tips with my small group, still bunkering tight in their homes. Days passed and no responses came. Not sure if the thumbs up emoji conveyed attendance.

Then it occurred to me: *I guess my friends won't have any problems when they retire.* Then my wife and I remembered one of her co-worker's plans to retire when she reaches her seventies. She needed more resources to finish her house being built in the Philippines.

Another friend came to mind. He decided to retire early by taking a buy-out from his employer—$250,000 + was a big money. He took it even before he turned fifty and rented a new condo in the belt line. Less than ten years of bliss and then we heard he was depressed. Rent and bills piling up. No job to sustain his life. Wife was working at a low-paying job.

Then I recalled our seminar facilitator. Pre-retirement planning isn't only for workers who are contemplating retiring. It's also for those early in their employment journey.

CIRCLE BACK

Many of my friends asked me years back why I'd moved to Canada with my family. Freedom and opportunity. Freedom to express your thoughts and opinions, engage in society, and decide what kind of political platform to support. Opportunity to improve your lot and be a positive member of the community. These two elements were in very short supply in the 1990s in our home country.

Thirty years passed in the land of milk and honey, and my experience and observations were haunting us. If your thoughts and opinions went against the government, you would be in big trouble. Now, after three years in the pandemic, your very livelihood and savings were threatened. It was no longer about COVID per se but about your civic position relative to the government's mandating what kind of life you could have here.

People elected them to work for us, not for us to follow their own interpretation of what is moral and right.

Now I'm in a position of circling back after thirty years. Unbelievable but true. I removed myself from the bondage of slavery to the land of freedom, and now the process has swung back to slavery. Your thoughts, opinions, actions, and resources are now being censored, and you could be cancelled.

CREATION AND MASKING

Who would think that masking was part of creation? The pandemic has proven it. Without the design of our ears, where would we hang our mask? Clever and smart human design. My ears are not big enough to handle double masks, though.

CRAZY GLUE

One Thursday morning, my officemate was prepping for his weekend skiing. He brought his skis into the office for tune-up: oil, screwdriver, wrench, and glue. I didn't bother to ask what the glue was for. Minutes into his prepping, he grabbed the glue on top of the table, opened it, and dropped a bit on his finger.

"It's not coming out. What kind of glue is this?" he asked in his frustrated voice.

I said, "It says clearly on the label."

He looked at it and said, "Yup, you are correct. It's a crazy glue."

VOLUNTEER

I thought millennials weren't impacted by the Russian invasion of Ukraine, but during one late-night talk with my daughter, out of nowhere she said, "Dad, I think we need to volunteer in Ukraine."

"What do you mean?" I asked.

She was toying the idea of going to the frontline to fight the invaders. Our eyes met. We looked at our tummies and burst into laughter.

"We'll not only be casualties there," I said, "but they'll categorize us as a liability. How could they ever supply our daily food? Besides, no more Netflix or cell phone for watching Tik Tok and FB."

"And the most important thing," she added, "no more asking you to help me wake up in the morning!"

She's turning twenty-nine. Duh!

LESSON LEARNED

A well-established businessperson in the Philippines, Garry (not his real name), and his family moved to Calgary a decade ago. It didn't take long for him to explore many business options. First on his list was food and feed supplements. The abundance of agricultural raw materials was his main reason for this choice. My experience, work, and network in Canadian agriculture helped him see the potential. His financial resources were solid, and the markets, based on his initial study in Alberta, seemed not to be a problem. Research was done, connections established, and sources of raw materials identified.

For whatever reason, his business idea didn't take off. The enormity of requirements and barriers to compete with the big and established corporations were concerning. These were draining him physically and, to some degree, financially. The lesson learned was that his brief exposure and dealing with the system weren't enough to thrust him to his dream of having a food and feed manufacturing plant.

Then came the networking. Another friend of mine, who was engaged in the manufacturing and sale of essential oils, crossed paths with Garry, so Garry took the opportunity to be one of the distributors in the Northern Alberta region.

The distributor's fee and the cost of inventory were part of the challenge. Sales weren't as good as projected, and the cost of his travel, food, and accommodation was more than his sales and collection per travel. Nevertheless, he saw the potential of the business. It was like his business in the Philippines.

He wanted to learn more about the essential oil business, and the lesson he learned from a course he took gave him hope.

Eventually, his relationship with the essential oils company went sour. Distrust ensued. Money matters made things worse. He parted with the owners, fuming. Thousands of dollars went unrecouped. Lawyers got involved. Court hearings were scheduled. The judge's ruling was laid down. Animosity went through the roof. True to his passion, though, Garry established his own essential oils business. Another lesson he learned—to stand his ground and deal with business partners with facts and credibility.

Another couple entered the scene. They convinced Garry to organize group of investors, and another essential oils business sprouted up. Garry was one of the founders. His plant would produce another line of the product's brand name. Many invested in the new venture, and the grand opening of the office was classy.

I wasn't invited, but I went as a member of the media, and Garry was surprised to see me at the event. I wished him well and good luck, and said the same to the other couple, Garry's business partners, whom I have known longer than Garry.

Months into the business, the operation hit a snag. A misunderstanding and a misappropriation of a promised commission came to the surface. The majority of the investors/business associates were asking about revenue, profit, and commissions, but the explanations were vague and misunderstood. Sales dwindled and needed boosting. Less than two years in operation, a legal battle brewed.

Things became even more complicated. Legal matters with the first couple-partners were still ongoing. Then another legal issue was brewing with the new group. Garry was at the centre of it all. Another lesson learned. Partnering with other Filipino entrepreneurs often required discernment and good judgement.

Then the COVID-19 pandemic entered the scene. Business operations were altered and impacted. The legal mess stagnated. Isolation made Garry's family more cohesive and closer. Business was still moving, but slowly and with caution.

Lessons on getting along with the in-laws posed more psychological challenges for Garry. Russian in-laws are different. The food, the way they do things, and many more aspects kept him on his toes. Over the years it went well, though.

One day Garry was deep in contemplation. Looking years ahead, he realized the importance of giving his kids the language tools to deal with relationships and business in the Philippines, so he enrolled them at the Filipino Language School somewhere on the northeast side of the city. Months passed, and their newfound language skills were just under the passing mark. That would suffice, Garry contended. Engaging with his children was a lesson worth pursuing.

Garry levelled up his biking skills. His stamina for long walks improved. Keeping pace with his kids was imperative. The same was true with his wife's lifestyle of sportsmanship and healthy food choices.

Garry taught his wife the basics of cooking adobo. Presto! His wife and kids liked it. However, Garry wasn't that enthusiastic about the menu. Lean pork was not to his taste. His palate always craved that half-inch-thick fat and a little bit of soy sauce.

From there, out of the lessons learned, life for Garry stabilized as he got used to more of the same routine—family, career, business, and relationships.

In the middle of the 2021–2022 winter, the government suspended most health directives. One weekend Garry's family went skiing in Sunshine Village. Truth be told, it was Garry's first time. His very first run didn't go well. He fell sideways and strained both thighs. A bit of regret, but he was determined to learn skiing for his kids' sake.

Aside from the book on skiing he was planning to buy, he was determined to take a lesson. But I said, "You learned your lesson the hard way last time, right?

"Not the kind of lesson I was talking about, Ka Romy," he answered.

We all LOL!

The last time we talked, I learned that he was diversifying his business to other product brands. Garry was and still is a man of many lessons.

MISCOMMUNICATION

Students went back to school. Pandemic mandates were still on. Programming and coordinating roles increased and were more frequent.

One big project was the awarding of recognition to outstanding student volunteers. It was the second time for Di (my daughter) to work on this project.

The first year was no hassle.

One week she felt terribly sad and frustrated. Di had forwarded a job request to the university's communications department for editing and publishing. The new person in charge of the process assured her that the job request had gone through, and everything would be fine. Tuesday was the publication release date, so Di followed up to confirm if everything was ok.

There was a snag. The material sent in needed reworking. Di stayed four hours into the evening to rectify the problem. The coms person couldn't do it because of the time constraints—it was the weekend.

Di emailed her concern to the head editor (the person Di had a hassle-free service request from the year before). In the ensuing correspondence, the new person's alibi was that there was miscommunication along the way.

On Monday morning the issue was tackled by Di and her supervisor. Di even got some sympathy from her colleague in the Faith and Spirituality Department, saying that "the new person was not that forthright. She always makes miscommunication an alibi."

A staff member from the communications department with a problem with communication. It's absurd and odd. Di wondered if the pandemic had something to do with this incident.

Fortunately, at the last hour, the problems were fixed. The following day, the materials were published, and everyone was relieved.

BREAK-IN

Months after the new alarm system in the office was installed, my workmate reminded me to arm it before leaving every Friday. Out of habit, I wasn't doing it because I just left it to the cleaners to arm the device.

Weeks later, the new security alarm provider reminded my mate to do just that—arm the alarm every Friday. No worries. It's no big deal. The first Friday after the reminder, I complied. The second Friday I forgot. No reminder from the provider.

Early Sunday morning, though, while prepping breakfast, my phone buzzed. My workmate had just gotten back from a weeklong holiday. Usually his calls were about being sick or coming in late. This time he said, "The office was broken into." I skipped my breakfast, drove fast, and arrived at the office.

I took a picture of the opened drawers, back door, and cabinets. It turned out the only thing missing was the old microscope that we seldom used. I noticed in our office supply storage room that the one-ton, heavy steel safe was there and locked. I worried about the cash in the safe. In our last estimate, there was over a hundred dollars cash in there.

The following morning, Monday, emails from our head office security officer flooded our mailbox with a series of questions and a request for pictures. The thing we dreaded most was the amount of paperwork and the reports the incident would entail—more paperwork than reporting a COVID incident.

That was the thing that would bother us most—the paperwork.

KEPT US WONDERING

The first half of the morning the following day was spent checking out everything that was out of the ordinary. We confirmed to our security guys in Winnipeg that the only thing missing was a microscope. Our computer systems and equipment were intact and not compromised, sabotaged, or damaged. Nothing was attached to our terminal, like a USB or other unfamiliar gadgets.

If not for a little wondering, our normal was back. The back door where the thief or thieves had entered wasn't damaged, and there were no marks of a forced entry. Something caught our attention, though. The metal back doorknob of our office is at the right side. However, two big slide-bolt door latches are attached at the left side of the door. It took us time to comprehend why that was so. It made no sense that such locks were installed on that side of the door. We slid the lock pin and opened the door. No use at all. The door opened perfectly.

Three days later, the building's maintenance guy came over and installed a new deadbolt lock. I took the opportunity to ask him about the two big slide-bolt latches. Only then did I understand. He explained and demonstrated to me the use of said latches. The door can be opened even without a key. The thief could remove the pin of the door hinges located at the outside of the door. Once the pins are removed, the door is compromised. It would take less than five minutes to do it.

It would be unfair to blame the pandemic for my innocence. My mind was focused only on what was obvious and could be properly argued. This time I saw the total picture of how security measures in doors are considered. That was enlightening.

EQUIPMENT INVENTORY LIST

The microscope that was taken during the break-in had been on top of the drawer for over fifteen years. Its model, serial number, sticker, and other identifying marks weren't part of our daily items to remember.

An email came listing the things we needed to prepare for the Zoom meeting. The head office wanted to know the model, serial number, and sticker of the microscope. The item was gone, and the only way to get this information was from the Equipment Inventory List. We took the time to browse all our accessible drives. In no time we were looking at the list. We'd found it.

One funny item included in the list of files was the file "lesson learned." My mate clicked the file, and before us was a report from a company that had gone under. We learned something new. The people involved in data and info management haven't learned their lesson. What in the world was the record of a grain company doing under the Equipment Inventory List?

The report was filed in this drive in the middle of 2021 pandemic.

TEXT

He is very responsible about letting me know his whereabouts, if he's coming late to work, doing stuff, or scheduling a holiday. My officemate's texts work well.

One Tuesday morning I received another text. He was running late. Understandable, again. Fifteen after the hour, he arrived. As usual, his driving was good, and his night firehall stint was productive. They doused off a house fire in just over an hour. No casualties, but the damage was great.

He relayed his observation that while waiting for the red light to turn green, he saw a Tim Horton's across the street. In a brief time, he counted eight police cars in the parking lot.

I quipped that a new product would be on display. Timbits were very popular, and the company had collaborated with Justin Bieber and now had timbiebs. I was hoping to have a Tim's Bests on display soon. It should have been thought of many years back, right?

TIME

It was mid-March when Arleigh, a good friend of mine, phoned and invited us to the *La Traviata* opera at the Jubilee Auditorium. My wife and I couldn't say no. We invited our friend Lisa to take the extra ticket.

The plans and allocation of our time for that date were well laid out. At quarter to five we picked up Lisa. We arrived in front of Arleigh's place at exactly six. Our drive from his place to the Silver Inn Restaurant was just five minutes. We were among the few early customers.

The food smelled fresh. We ordered the usual Chinese menu we were familiar with. Our conversation was fun and insightful. Catching up and touching base in person brought a more pleasant encounter. Masks and distance mandates were gone. We left the Inn after a satisfying meal.

I turned to the north side parking lot of the auditorium. It was full, so the parking attendant directed us to the south side of the building. Indeed, we found a good spot.

People were in a hurry. Others were busy with their hand-held gadgets. Parking apps made their payment easy. Once we reached the main level of the building, we saw a long line of people. The four parking meter machines were manned by parking lot security.

The show would be starting in ten minutes.

I was in front of the machine and brought out my debit card, but the machine didn't read the card. I confirmed what I'd read. The machine didn't accept debit cards. I dug into my small wallet and inserted my newly-issued credit card. Five minutes to the show. I'd forgotten to reactivate the card days before.

I stepped aside so that people could pay for their parking. The reactivation procedure was automated. It took me five trials. Three minutes to the show. My card number was right. The expiration date was unrecognizable. Even the itching cough of my throat while relaying the numbers created a big snag. Back to redialing the number. Then it occurred to me. I shouldn't have said "oh" but "zero."

The snow started to fall when I finally got it. I was quite happy because another couple was in a hurry to purchase their parking ticket. The guy asked and I told him to get the max amount.

In my hurry, I wasn't even thinking properly. The lady ahead of me in the first door of the building leading to the auditorium couldn't open it. We thought when the opera started all doors would automatically lock up. I tried all the doors, and no luck. But then I tried pulling, not pushing, one of the doors. It opened. However, the lady manning the locked auditorium doors advised us to just wait for the intermission. I missed the first thirty minutes of the show, as did the couple, the lady, and many more sitting in the lobby.

After the intermission, I got inside the hall and found my spot. I narrated my experience to my friends. They all smiled. The opera went well.

I only had to read the captions on the screen to understand the flow of the story. I asked Arleigh why they didn't just sing in English so that there would be no need for the captions. Not to distract the people around us, I just nodded at his explanation.

The storyline was just the usual. Parents' instinct. Dad not in favour of his son's love life. The couple separated and, of course, at the end reunited momentarily. For whatever reason—joy, illness, or exhaustion— the leading lady dies at the hand of her lover. What a tragedy.

The crowd stood up and applauded the re-entrance of the cast. Just the same. A minute or two of appreciation. The clapping of the big guy behind us was deafening. Looked like a deluge of all his energy stored during the pandemic burst out that night.

The flow of people coming out of the hall was orderly. In no time we reached the parking lot. As we headed out of the compound, we talked again about the pandemic, Ukraine, summer plans, and church.

Arleigh said that their church started at ten in the morning. No more restrictions. He asked what time our group starts. I said, "Our service starts at 10:30, and we'll beat our record next Sunday by being there no later than 10:35!" We all "lol."

My stress from that parking ticket experience was gone. We got home on time as expected and went to bed, still reeling from what that opera was all about.

PHOTO OPS

The leadership review of Alberta's premier was slated for mid-May. Irma, one of the UCP foot soldiers, called me a day before a select gathering of party brass in the Glenmore Inn hotel.

The meeting started at one. I got into the half-full room at 1:10. The host welcomed the delegates and guests and acknowledged the old guard with care. Those with ministerial positions stood up with grace as their names were called. As usual, I took the back seat. I scanned the crowd and tried to locate Irma. Nope. I couldn't see her shadow.

After a short intro, then Premier Kenny, pumped up, climbed the stage. People stood and applauded. He talked about his government's accomplishments, first the lifting of health measures mandates, and then the robust economy (leading the country), investments in gas and green tech, and many more. Sounded impressive.

He also talked about the perceived division in the party, the discontent of a few that was infecting the party. The big issue was the change in the voting system for the leadership review, from in-person to mail-in ballots. It was argued that the opportunity of all party members to have their say heard weighed heavier than just those who would be attending in person. Looked convincing.

I seldom follow the political discourse of the province, so all the questions asked after the premier's talk were vague to me.

When the photo op started, I saw this woman heading in the direction of the premier. Following behind her was a man I didn't know. Irma was happy and asked where I'd been during the meeting. She'd been sitting in the front. She introduced to me her boyfriend, whose name didn't register well in my memory, as usual, I guess.

People gathered around trying to get a moment of the premier's time for a photo op. After minutes of pleasantries, Irma asked if I wanted to have a photo taken with Jason. From nowhere I said, "If the premier wanted to have a photo op with me, then I'd be ok." Irma stared at me for a second and a half. I don't know what was in her mind, but her smile came back and she dragged the premier from his conversation with the other people. I'm not sure if the short introduction was enough for Jason to remember the Filipino guy in front of him. I handed my cell phone to Irma, who took just one shot of me and the premier. The shot was sharp and clear.

As we left the building, Irma encouraged me to participate and engage in political advocacy in the province. The idea sounded exciting to me. I told her to just give me a shout if there was something I could do to help. Since then, I haven't heard from her.

I showed my wife the picture taken with the premier. She warned me not to show it to our daughter. We're both aware that our daughter's political leaning is opposite to the one we embrace. A typical millennial, my daughter was working at the University's Women's Resource Centre. Clashes of the titans in the family, as I called it, were common.

While talking about my time at the premier's meeting, my daughter appeared from the back door. I intentionally shifted our conversation to what had happened to our office. I handed my cell phone to my daughter and showed her the photos I'd taken at the office.

She scanned and stared at the photos—open drawers, the empty tabletop where the microscope had been located, etc. Then she said, "Why?"

"Why what?" I followed up her question.

She was referring to my photo op with the premier. My reasoning wasn't enough to convince her. I stuck to my story, and she stuck to her opinion about the governing party.

The pandemic, the office break-in, and the lifting of health mandates became peripheral issues that whole evening—clashing of the titans in a mannered, civil, and do-as-you-please moment.

One lesson I learned, though, during that meeting earlier that day was a familiar quotation: "Don't compare me with the almighty. Compare me with the alternatives."

Like the premier's leadership, the pandemic mandates elicited differing contentions and opinions. The more perspective and opinions floating around the more the truth was being left and hidden behind.

Weeks later, the premier got just over 50 per cent in a party confidence vote. He stepped down as the leader and premier.

Our photo op was memorable and historic, I guess.

SPAM TO SCAM

The thought of food shortages brought a chill to many, my daughter included. To mitigate the anxiety, we drove to Walmart one day. Quality came secondary. Price was supreme. Among the items we carted out was this low-priced SPAM made in Denmark. Almost half the price of the leading one.

Saturday morning I took on my normal chef's role: friend rice, eggs, and SPAM to brighten the day of my wife and daughter. I heard nothing from my wife about the menu I prepared that morning. It was about noon when my daughter woke up and smelled the food on the table. The first bite was normal. Her second try for the SPAM made her eyes roll.

"Dad!" she said loudly. "Where did you buy this SPAM? It tastes awful!"

I let her words sink into my head. They were followed by, "This is not a SPAM."

"What then?" I responded.

"It's a scam."

I guess she has a point.

EVERY MOVING THING

In mid-March, the Calgary Zoo reported that five hundred animals had been jabbed with the COVID vaccine.

It wouldn't be long before the COVID vaccine found its way to the livestock industry.

I wonder if these big pharma companies were designing vaccines for all agricultural crops and animals known to humans. Or were they planning to develop a vaccine for all moving and living things.

Our health is their wealth.

SEDATION

The instructions about the procedures were clear and comprehensive.

I arrived in the facility confident that I'd followed all the requirements. Minutes into the reception area, the attending nurse led me to another room. There I undressed. The gown covering my body was big for my size. Hmm. Before she inserted a needle into my right arm, I warned her. The average number of pokes to get the blood from my veins was three. I asked her also if she could use a baby needle. She just smiled. Nope, she said. She beat the record. One poke indeed. Blood flowed out to the vial. She told me that she'd put saline solution into the plastic tube attached to the syringe stuck into my arm. I felt nothing after the saline was injected.

I observed four other persons wheeled out from the operating room. All were motionless. From the same room came the attending doctor. She walked to my bed, introduced herself, and asked if I preferred to be sedated. It sounded comforting to me. I said yes. She said sedation was the common preference of most people undergoing a colonoscopy. I looked around and saw that the people around me had started to show movement.

The nurse wheeled me off to the room, followed by the doctor. There was a big TV monitor hanging at the east side wall. I scanned the little room curiously. The time was 9:45, forty-five minutes after I'd checked in at the reception desk. I followed the instruction to position myself sideways with my legs folded like a baby.

The nurse, with a syringe of the sedative, took hold of the vial hanging from my right hand and injected the sedative. Without a warning or a word, the doctor started to insert the tube into my basement sewer. At first, I felt something. That was the last thing I remember.

A tap on my shoulder woke me up. I looked at the time, and it was 10:30. The nurse asked me to proceed to the washroom, metres away from my bed, to clean up, and to put on my mask to be safe. The first few steps were groggy. I swerved a little but managed to walk properly. There was nothing to worry about. There was no trace of irregularity, either blood spots or pain.

Before I put on my clothes, the nurse offered me a snack. I chose apple juice and crackers. Twenty-four hours of no food was a challenge. In less than one minute, I consumed the snack. I smiled.

I called my daughter to pick me up at the same spot where she'd dropped me off earlier that day. My plan to grab a hamburger along the way didn't materialize, as she had to go back to work at once. So I settled for left-over food at home.

During dinner the next day, my wife and daughter asked what it was like to be sedated. I shared that it was one of the best medical procedures I'd ever had. I was in a deep sleep for thirty minutes and didn't even feel anything during the procedure.

"How's that possible?" they inquired.

It was 9:45 when I was sedated. My everyday (regular) nap time starts at 9:50.

We all lol!

HOT WATER?

My daughter is an advocate of drinking hot water. She's convinced that hot water is good for one's health. It's a common practice for the Chinese elderly. No argument there, I guess. It's been my habit ever since. Masking, distancing, and hot water drinking were part of my everyday pandemic routine at home and at the workplace.

One time my workmate saw me consume lots of hot water. In the office we have a hot water dispenser (aside from microwave, toaster, ref, and other appliances). Out of curiosity, he asked, "Why do you drink hot water?"

I was caught off guard and couldn't find a quick answer, so I responded, "My wife and daughter told me to drink hot water because I'm getting older and getting colder now."

"Oh, I see," he quipped.

DOORBELL

After the break-in at our office, the alarm company visited us. Security decals were left for us to stick to the doors. Days later, the building maintenance guy made a routine check and figured out what things needed to be fixed. The back door, where the thief presumably entered, needed attention. A dead bolt was installed. Next in line was the stop plate along the locks. The last job was to change the location of the doorbell.

Originally, the doorbell was at the right side of the door, opposite to the opening of the door. The maintenance guy decided to move it to the left side of the door for easier access. He cut the old line but forgot to bring new ones, so he postponed the installation for the day. Hours after he'd left the building, we heard loud bangs at the back door. Scott jumped and opened it. Outside was this FedEx guy with a bunch of deliveries.

For the next two years of the pandemic, no one used the back door for delivery. There will always be intended consequences of the pandemic—the break-in, fixing stuff, and the wrong-door delivery.

SELFIE

During the pandemic, I had various procedures done. The X-ray result of my right knee indicated a light to moderate form of rheumatoid arthritis. My doctor told me that he couldn't issue a handicap sign for parking yet. No luck there.

Months later, my doctor issued a requisition for another procedure. The lingering pain over my chest was more stress than muscle spasm. The pills worked well over a period of time, and I worried less and minimized thinking about unnecessary stuff.

My glaucoma needed laser surgery. Both eyes were scheduled weeks apart. The procedures were a success. My eye doctor showed me the before and after image of my inner eyes.

Months later, another concern cropped up. This time my eye doctor scheduled cataract removal with a few weeks in between the eyes. It gave me hope and pleasure that after this procedure my appetite and passion for reading would be back to normal. A pure pleasure on the horizon.

My last lower left molar became an enemy. When I saw the X-ray result, I asked my dentist to extract it. In no time I went home with my half my face numbed.

Less than a week later, another member, now in front of the row, was badly affected by the harsh nature of hard-to-chew food passing by. The chipped portion was not presentable. Though wearing a mask was a blessing in disguise, the need for repair was called for. My dentist didn't have the equipment or tools to do the job, so referral would be the best option. And it would cost me a lot.

Dr. Mary had been a friend for many years, so I sought her opinion. The following week, I discussed with her the procedures needed to make my denture look natural so that I wouldn't fear showing off my inherently beautiful smile. I asked her how much it would cost, less my insurance coverage. My knee, chest, eyes, and mouth went numb. The X-ray revealed that a total renovation was required, including bridge construction, underground drilling, post reinforcement, and possibly all types of procedures known to the dental industry. When she showed the cost estimate, I thought of selling my other car. I promised to get back to her later that week. But it took me weeks of study and contemplation to reach a decision. As of this writing, I haven't decided yet what to do. One thing is sure though—I still have boxes of masks at home, possibly good for another year. Well, another year of a hidden smile and agonizing chew.

As I took a stock of my pandemic health procedures, it occurred to me that my body parts clamoured for their own selfie. Their selfie manifested honesty, loyalty, no pretension, authenticity, and no faking around.

CONCERT HALL

Leah Salonga is one of the most popular singers/performers in the Philippines. Her scheduled concert in Calgary the first week of April 2022 was a hit.

From the main floor to the third floor, our ascent took minutes. The foot traffic was heavy, and the movement of people slow. At last, we sat in our respective spot.

Moments later, a lady came looking for her chair. Our friendliness sparked a good conversation. To our dismay, she mentioned that one of her friends who was coming had tested positive. I wasn't convinced by her reassuring word that she'd be getting out of the hall when her friend arrived. Moments later, a throng of people came in, eyeing in our direction. We were in the very last row. Five vacant seats were waiting for them. Our newly-found worried friend was seriously looking to see if one of the people coming our way was her positive housemate. Nope. We all breathed a sigh of relief.

Minutes before the start of the show, people took their selfies. Selfies in all directions. We could only do it with the stage as the background. We were sitting in the very last row, and there's no point taking selfie with a background of a dry, egg-shell-white coloured wall. The cheapest, farthest, and most obscured spot in the Jack Singer Concert Hall.

INCOMPLETE

The sudden passing of a staff member in our head office in Winnipeg brought sadness and magnified the seriousness and malady of mental health. Three children and a spouse were left grieving. We were all advised to seek support from and/or counselling through the Employee Assistance Program (EAP). We were also directed to talk to our immediate supervisor.

Two days after the news, our supervisor called in. We talked operational and inspections stuff. Our performance evaluation was also discussed. At the end of the discussion, we were asked how we were doing. My mate, in his usual way and with no hesitancy, shared his family, part-time work, and career challenges. Methodically he shared concerns that greatly affected his wellbeing. His adult children's challenges of living by themselves. His daughter's boyfriend's foot was infected. The leaking waterline in the laundry area of the apartment his daughter was renting was a big concern. He was stressed over his son's parking and speeding tickets. They amounted to hundreds of dollars. The passing of his aunt, cousin, and friend was despairing. His retirement plan and the issue of where to move gave him sleepless nights. His wife's workplace turmoil was another frustrating story. He shared details of the issues engulfing his part-time job as a fireman. And many more issues and concerns.

"Don't you have any thoughts of suicide?" asked our supervisor.

"Nope," he answered. "Romy is around. He's my shock absorber."

We finished with a deeper understanding of how mental health should be addressed properly.

Later in the day, as we continued to digest the impact of our friend's passing, my mate remembered two or three more important issues he'd failed to mention during our call.

I admonished him and said, "Don't worry about the incomplete story." Then it occurred to us that life must go on amid pandemic and post-pandemic. The incompleteness of our daily life story and narrative will come to full view somewhere, somehow, sometime.

CALL SCAM

Twice or thrice a week I receive a call at either ten in the morning or three in the afternoon from unknown numbers. I tried one time to answer and, presto, it was a scam call.

What was positive about these calls was that they shortened my nap time. So I'm a bit thankful, though I never answered a scam call again.

I call it a wake-up call.

MALPRACTICE

The house blessing of one of my friends was a blast. Over twenty people came. All were excited to see the new place they'd just moved into. The house was just a five-minute walk away from the newly-built East Hill Shopping Centre on the east side of Calgary.

A couple was in the crowd, Chris and his wife, whom I hadn't seen for over three months. He's older than me by two weeks. The bulk of our talk revolved around retirement. His decision was final, but I sensed that his wife wasn't totally sold on the idea. They still had a mortgage, and their adult son was still living with them, and he didn't earn enough to pay the bills.

In our sharing, tension between the couple bubbled up, so I switched the focus of our conversation. I asked Chris how his mom was doing in the Philippines. He'd gone back home to the Philippines months ago due to his mom's condition. At ninety-six, her vision had deteriorated. He convinced his mom to have her eyes checked, and in no time, both eyes were cleared of cataracts. Chris was very thankful the procedures had been successful. In their monthly video chat, his mom always mentioned how good-looking Chris was.

The aura of the couple's uneasiness lingered in the air. To fully defuse the situation, I jokingly advised Chris to sue the doctor who'd attended to his mom. He surprisingly asked, "What for?"

"You mom's eyesight wasn't properly cured," I said, "or your mom's not telling the truth. It's an issue of malpractice. To prove it, look in the mirror when you got back home." Our friends listening to our conversation around the table LOL.

The couple left the house with the assurance that they would attend our pre-retirement seminar.

IF THE PRICE IS RIGHT

As of June 16, 2022, my team, Diaryo Alberta Society, has distributed over 2,200 certificates of recognition and appreciation and gift bags to COVID-19 pandemic heroes in Alberta. Our generous sponsors are comprised of private colleges and businesses. Without them, that number would not have been reached.

On the last Saturday of June 2022, we held an appreciation brunch. Five schools in one gathering seemed a daunting task for us to pull off. We worried about the impression each school would have if we put them together under one roof.

We took the chance. Our approach was carefully prepared. In my introduction, I said, "Our society is a neutral, fair, balanced, unbiased, impartial, and imperfect society. We entertain any organization, business, political party, and/or professional practitioner looking for promotional help from us." Then I added, "As long as the price is right."

All laughed a good, healthy laugh.

At the end of the gathering, I presented to them the proof of our imperfection. We presented their certificate of appreciation separate from the frame, as the size of the frame was smaller than the certificate itself. They got it, and our honesty was well appreciated. The following week, the framed certificates were distributed to them.

Part of the plan was to ascertain their comfort level interacting with other competitor schools. All manifested civility. I substantiated it with a group dynamic, and I asked everyone to join in the game of untangle, which was well received. It was new to them. At the end, they all appreciated the lesson. They created a circle out of tangled hands holding each other. I called it the circle of career and academic influencers in Calgary.

We all hoped to have this idea materialize in the very near future. All approved of the idea.

We all left the room maskless and without mentioning the pandemic. Quite a relief to be free from that little obstruction in one's face. All smiles were seen, and all laughs were heard and not muffled.

MY TURN

The lifting of public health mandates added more life and energy to people as they headed to spring outdoor adventures. Including me. Scheduled meeting attended. Pageantry, small group and business meetings, welcome dinner, and many other appointments—doctor and dental—accomplished.

Days after my dentist fixed two of my front teeth, my zest for smiling intensified. Mask no more inside or outside any facility. I thought my cautiousness had paid off. For the last thirty-eight months, never did I get a cold, sinus infection, flu, or COVID. Quite a record of being safe, I thought. Daily dose of vitamins, six hours of sleep, good nutrition, masking, distancing, and below par body activity (this is where I planked) shielded me from the creepy COVID.

April showers bring May flowers, as the saying goes, and April exposure makes May risk bigger. Presto! In mid-May my rapid test resulted to two red marks. The two jabs I took proved less effective. Instead of having my booster, as demanded by my wife and daughter, I resorted to booster juice.

At first the symptoms were common flu-like. Days later, my noodles tasted and smelled the same—bland and stale. Aching muscles, headache, fever, and irritated throat were noticeable. Advil provided short-term relief.

On the third day I experienced loss of not only appetite but taste and smell. Jogging nose turned to running. Coughing to barking. Red line was established. The living room became my sanctuary and castle. I said goodbye to Mr. Ad Vil and welcomed Mr. Ty Lenol Extra Fort.

Mr. Ty's suppressant capability worked well. Oversleep added to my head's disorientation. More fluid intake resulted in more litres flushed. Netflix remained my loyal and reliable friend. Its 24/7 provision of time-wasting programs opened my eyes to weirder, out of this world ideas and life stories.

A friend of mine called one night. Her surprise was obvious and her concern sounded like a well-trained pharmacist and experienced medical doctor. One leaf of oregano (herb) per glass of water intake gave her the welcomed hour-long relief.

I checked my indoor plants. The leaves of the oregano seemed to be waving and smiling at me. The knife was sharp, and it pained me to cut off one of the leaves. I folded the leaf into four and poured boiling water into a cup with the leaf. What a relief, indeed. In two days, what remained on the slender, fragile stalk were three young leaves at the tip of the growth. It looked like it had been visited by the pandemic.

I realized my wife liked the idea of separation during that time of my positivity. Even my daughter was hesitant to even have a brief conversation with me. I needed to keep my distance, my hands washed, and my mask on. While having these relational challenges, my internal elements were calling for attention. After a glass of hot water and a small measure of solid food, my tummy started to churn. Gastrointestinal pain seemed like bloating and indigestion at the same time. Less than an hour of sleep on the fourth night. Power of mind was no match to the power of COVID, I guess.

I've proven and experienced that having the illness is no fun. It robbed me of time, joy of interaction with my loved ones, fellowship with friends, church, colleagues, and co-workers. It also kept me away from my daily chores at home. Cool.

From intellectual understanding of the pandemic to experiential encounter, it reinforced my perception, observations, and experiences about being one of the members of humanity. The pandemic was one of the great equalizers. Each person has a unique and interesting story to tell.

HERITAGE MONTH

Both the governments of Canada and Alberta declared June as the Philippines' Heritage Month. Over a million Filipinos celebrated this event with fanfare. Months of preparation yielded so many events. Food festivals, fashion shows, cultural presentations, sports, fitness demonstrations, and many more events were notedly enjoyed by the mainstream society.

Our society, Diaryo Alberta, invited the first Filipino woman Member of Parliament. The Hon. Rechie Valdez agreed to visit Alberta to grace and cap off the celebration. Her three-day visit was historical.

Her flight arrived two hours late. People at the meeting venue, Barrio Restaurant, were understanding. Minutes after reading her arrival text, I proceeded to where she was waiting. Very few were wearing masks at the arrival terminal. She directed me to proceed to gate # 9. My wife and I were waiting at gate # 2.

From a distance I could see her checking her phone. No mistaking, it was her with a smile. I grabbed her luggage and had her occupy the front seat. A minute of pleasantries and greetings established our rapport.

The traffic outside the airport wasn't heavy. The scheduled start of the meeting was 11:00. We arrived forty-five minutes past the time. However, guests and visitors (around fifty) were happy to meet Rechie.

After changing her attire into a Filipino barong, the program started. Marietta, the host of the event, navigated and modified the program with ease.

Two newly formed groups (officers) from far north of the province were inducted and challenged.

One part of the program turned emotional. Tears fell down Rechie's cheeks when she received the white hat as a symbol of her adoption as a Calgarian. The same emotion showed up when gifts like a certificate of honorary membership to our society and many other items were handed over to her.

The photo ops lasted minutes short of one hour.

Our next leg of travel was Canmore, the town before Banff National Park. It was Rechie's third visit to the park. It had been her first time in Calgary hours ago.

As we threaded our way along the valley into the side of the mountains, her amazement was pronounced. She commented that her riding in Mississauga-Streetsville has no area like this. I believed her.

Sheila and Edwin were the couple waiting for us. We talked about our (my wife and I) accommodation in town. Rechie's staff had booked her hotel in Banff. When she heard that a motorhome parked in one of the camp sites close to McDonald's was waiting for us, Rechie insisted on joining us. We couldn't believe her decision. I could drive her to Banff and pick her up anytime. We couldn't resist her wish.

The couple led us to the motorhome, where we unpacked and made ourselves relax and rest. Minutes later my phone rang. The group at the Quatro Restaurant was there waiting for us. In no time we met them checking out the food menu. Greetings, more greetings, and introductions ensued.

The food was superb. The exchanges were pleasant, and our itinerary for the next day looked great.

Back to the motorhome. The first half of the night was warm. Around two or three in the morning, though, the temperature dropped too low. We were worried for Rechie. It was our first time sleeping in a motorhome, so I never asked about the thermostat. One thing for sure, we knew that Rechie was trying to keep herself warm by curling up hard. At around

7:30, she begged us to turn on the thermostat. I called Sheila, who told me that the thermostat was located at the base of the television. I found it. Our guest stayed in her bed for another ten minutes. Enough time to warm the motorhome.

When we entered the buffet lounge of the Canmore Inn and Suite twelve, leaders stood up and greeted us enthusiastically. Greetings, more greetings, and introductions. Moments later, we enjoyed the cereals, oatmeal, eggs, sausages, yogurts, coffee, juices, pancakes, etc. — the usual hotel breakfast.

The first room booked for our meeting was small, so the manager led us to a bigger room on the third floor, overlooking the majesty and beauty of the Rockies. A formal introduction was the first item on the agenda. Business owners and community leaders proudly shared their stories. Rechie, the last one, delved into her message after introducing herself. So much inspiration and encouragement in the room. Promises were less said than expected. However, Rechie was committed to exploring and finding answers to the groups' inquiries and questions.

After the meeting, we proceeded outside for a group photo op. Contact numbers were exchanged, and I saw the taillights of my car in the parking lot. Our next destination was Banff. However, one of the key people in the group insisted that we go around Canmore for a quick tour. He said there was one spot seldom visited by tourists. Only local folks visit the place for serenity, calm, and beauty.

We ended up in one cul-de-sac and walked for five minutes until we saw the Engine's Bridge in front of us. We'd visited Canmore many times but had never heard about this bridge. Indeed, the scenery was awesome. Rechie paused here and there, a little bit further on and closer to the edge, etc. By her amazement we believed she savoured and stored all the memories she could grasp in the moment.

As we left the bridge, a plan materialized. We were invited to check out the Quarry Lake, a few minutes' drive from the Canmore town proper, after the event in Banff. The lake was one of the nicest spots in town. But due to fatigue and stress, we couldn't join. Jing, one of the key leaders in Canmore, would pick up Rechie from our camp site for a walk around the lake early in the evening.

Our Engine Bridge rendezvous ended around noon and off we drove to Banff National Park.

Finding a parking spot is one of the chronic problems that plagued the town. Before heading off, I recalled Edwin's advice. I followed the directions and safely parked the car on the third level of the city's public parking. Parking along the street in town wasn't free, but up to where I got the spot was free and just metres away from the venue of the Banff's Taste of Culture Festival.

Scattered at the back of the Whyte Museum were booths from five ethnic communities. The Philippines tent provided the greatest amount of food to the crowd. Attended by over 250 folks, the event was made lively by various ethnic performances. As usual, the Filipino dance group, Maharlika, proved entertaining. The host was excited to announce that someone from Ottawa had arrived to grace the event.

Rechie took the mic and shared her thoughts on the importance of community and collaboration. The unified efforts of all levels of government were the cornerstone of social cohesion and strength. Her presence made us all proud, to the point that people flocked our tent and asked for more food servings.

Rechie made more connections and friends in the community. She expressed her concern for the Indigenous group. The shirts she bought from an Indigenous artist were a good example of this.

Though the sun was still up and shining hot, the organizers prodded each community exhibitor to pack up. The show would be over in just a few minutes.

Our free time was spent on a quick tour of Banff Spring Golf Course, where our society planned to hold our next year's food gala. We indicated to Rechie that the event would be best if she could be our VIP guest. Without any hint of hesitation, she said yes.

It was late, but the sun was still up when we reached our camp site. As previously agreed upon earlier, Jing picked up Rechie and both headed out to Quarry Lake. An hour later, like a kid with a curfew, Rechie sneaked into the motorhome silently at around ten o'clock. We pretended to be soundly sleeping by our moderated snoring.

Our second night was comfortable, and not because of the thermostat. The temperature outside was warm, so there was no need for it inside. At around seven, however, Rechie, from her bed, requested that we turn on the heat. We complied, and minutes later she bolted out of her cocoon. Sheila and Edwin's beaming smiles added spark to our morning. The McDonalds b-fast combos with the hot coffee on the park table outside the motorhome were perfect.

We informed our hosts of our plan to travel to Red Deer and Edmonton. The couple's generosity was evident. We were given bags of gifts. Hugs and farewells ensued, and then they left us for their daily work routine. We checked out, walked to our car, and looked back at the motorhome. History had been made, and quite possibly for Rechie as Member of Parliament, who had officially travelled in the west. We were glad to be part of her humanity as she joined us in a motorhome. We wondered if the same experience was had by her colleagues in Ottawa.

I wasn't sure if I'd made the wrong turn. I thought I'd followed the right route, but it took us over three hours navigating the back country highways to get to our destination. One lady from the venue, Barkada Grill in Red Deer, called and asked our time of arrival. Upon hearing about our situation, they said they could stay put and wait for us. I put in one more hour on the road. We reached the place with only five people inside—leaders and key people of the Filipino group in Red Deer.

The meeting was cordial, and the food was great. Rechie heard some of the issues related to the federal government's programs on immigration and related mandates. She promised to bring the matter to the minister in charge of the issue.

The photo ops were short, and then we boarded our car and hit the road. An hour and a half had been added to our trip. Rechie requested that we drop by and see one of her social media friends in Edmonton. The owners of Yelo'd Ice Cream and Bake Shoppe were so happy to meet Rechie in person, and their ice cream was superb. I forget what Rechie ordered. We even visited their store in the inner Strathcona area. I looked at the time and indicated to her that people in the community hall, minutes away from the store, were waiting patiently for us. We left the store with a bag of cookies. Cool.

Around fifty people were enjoying their chit chats when we entered the room. Food on the tables was half consumed. I thought they'd been waiting on us. I grabbed a paper plate and put some items on it. Rechie didn't touch the food my wife had prepped for her.

After minutes of formal introductions, the questions raised were all valid and important. Rechie, to the best of her ability, assured them that concerns that had not been addressed would be forwarded to the appropriate minister once she was back to Ottawa.

It was late in the evening when everybody retreated. My responsibilities to Rechie ended when I initiated the hand-over ceremony. She pleaded with us to stay with her in her hotel that night, but we said sorry. The family who would be taking care of her stay in Edmonton opened their arms wide and welcomed Rechie warmly. I made sure a photo of this moment was taken. After she hugged everyone in the crowd, she stepped in my direction. We hugged tight and long. Her tear wetted part of my shoulder. She got into the waiting car crying. Once again, I witnessed her humility and humanity. Her authentic care for Filipinos was no secret, and her joyful demeanour and respect for everyone was infectious.

From the time we picked her up at the airport to the moment of her retreat inside the car of her newly-found foster parents, never once did we talk about the pandemic.

That was quite an experience in public service with one of the country's newly minted Members of Parliament.

OVERCOOKED
Occasionally I drove through the McDonalds on my way to work. Out of habit, I always ordered the breakfast meal combo # 8. Familiarity allowed a few moments of pleasantry with the old lady inside the till booth.

"So your wife forgot to cook your food this morning?" she teased me.

"Nope, the food was overcooked," I responded.

GARAGE SALE 1.0
My small group for years has been sending monthly financial support to Indigenous people on one of the islands in the Philippines, Mindoro.

Many months ago, the big box of stuff was just a memory. However, it gave us joy to see that some of the Natives wore the clothes we'd sent them.

When the pandemic struck, our giving slowed down, so we had to think of ways to level up the support again. I contacted the Bureau of Animal Industry in Manila to ask if we could send them ducks, chickens, rabbits, goats, and other sources of protein. The inquiry was attended to positively. The only problem was that we should be the ones picking up the animals from Manila and taking them to their location—four hours by boat. It would take days and large sums of money to facilitate this transfer.

The challenge was enormous. By the nature of their livelihood, the group moved from one place to another. The community has no permanency in terms of settlement.

Their need for more assistance was getting louder and clearer every day. Pictures on social media touched my group in Calgary. During our meeting, we discussed how to tackle the need expressed to us from the island. Out of many options presented, what stood out and was agreed upon was a garage sale. Each family was encouraged to set aside stuff (clothing, furniture, etc.) for this momentous event.

One day my wife was busy collecting and prepping all the items to be sold in the garage sale. The number seemed ample. A few dollars here and there would be great for our friends in the Philippines.

Days before our group set up the garage sale, the impact of inflation dominated the news. It was reported that the rate in the later weeks of July was the same as Canada had experienced almost forty years ago at 8.5 per cent. The prices of all consumer goods had gone up. Few dared to drive more than what was needed, as gas prices were prohibitive. Food prices went up to the roof.

The rate of the virus infection in some regions of Canada was also getting higher. The projection for the fall in terms of the eighth wave was scary.

Then it occurred to me to ask my wife, "What's the chance that our garage sale will yield better results? Our neighbourhood isn't one of the affluent communities in Calgary. Everyone has been affected by inflation. Do you think they can afford time and extra money to buy used items amid inflation?" I read my wife's mind as she just sighed.

I brought the boxes of items to the site of the garage sale early the next morning. By mid-morning, the driveway was full of stuff. People passing by on the sidewalk curiously stepped into the den of used items. Most of the guys were looking for tools; unfortunately, not even one was on display.

Hours passed and little by little the number of items thinned out. Roughly a third of the original display was intact and literally dispersed.

Mid-afternoon we decided to wrap up, pack up, and sort the stuff for give away to the local thrift store and landfill. After clearing out the driveway, we went into the house. The food on the table settled and gave us time to calm down and be refreshed.

While we were busy working on food, Fatima, one of the leading ladies, counted the money. After two or three counts, she announced with great pride the total sales of the day. Over $1,000.00—a record since our group had started garage sale many years back. What was left were three boxes full of clothing, shoes, and small items worth over a hundred dollars.

Our theory posited earlier was debunked. Even amid inflation, the number of items for sale at the almost give-away price made the difference. Still, buyers were very good at bargaining—the very essence of surviving garage sales.

Our day ended with a very insightful observation. Amid the pandemic, inflation, and quality items on display, people's propensity to make decisions based on price played a big role.

Like a vaccine of relief, the Indigenous people on the other side of the world were waiting with great anticipation. Barefooted children would have their shoes on going to school. Mothers would be proud doing their chores in town in their new suits. Their leaders would find great joy in bringing in needed support from the sale of the three boxes.

In a small, tangible, and lasting gesture of support, the impact of the pandemic and inflation in the lives of less fortunate Indigenous people, for a short period in their lives, was lessened.

STAMPEDE

The return of the Stampede (2022) in Calgary was welcomed with a blast. Previous attendance records were broken. Over a million attended. The record number was confirmed by our society's (Diaryo Alberta Society) own booth record. In our first three days, we logged over a thousand signatures of participants in our raffle draw.

Exposure-wise, our booth inside the BMO Centre was great. However, during our debriefing, one commentary cropped up. The first three days when the attendance was so high were the days of free entrance for seniors, families, kids, and the community.

We browsed the list and found a pattern. Over 90 per cent of the registrants' names were recognizably of Filipino origin.

The pandemic and inflation were no match to free entrance to the Stampede. Cool.

GARAGE SALE 2.0

He started working in his early teens. Last May 2022, my officemate reached his thirtieth year of service with the Canadian Grain Commission. "A few months' extension was not bad," he said.

Plans were drawn up. His wife and adult children, all working, couldn't care less. The major decisions to address concerned selling the house, choosing a city to move to, and the stress it would give to Tucker, their dog.

For two weeks my workmate and his wife drove to Okanagan, Penticton, and neighbouring interior British Columbia towns. Prices went high. Funds weren't enough. Too much hassle along the way. Their kids just shrugged their shoulders. "Forget it," he said about the plan of retiring in that part of Canada.

When his house was sold in August, he decided that mid-November would be his last day with the commission.

One Monday morning I asked, "How was your garage sale?"

After a second of silence, he said, "It was a waste of time. We shouldn't have done it." The couple had brought out all their garage-sale items to the front of their house. The front lawn was almost covered with items they'd accumulated over the fifteen years of their stay in Strathmore.

"Waste of time because the whole time only three people cared to check out the items displayed for sale," he said. "Only one item was taken away from the box full of free items!" He sighed with a look of sorrow on his face.

He promised not to move into another place again. He blamed the beautiful weather and COVID.

ONE MISSING

Months after retirement, my wife's connection with her workplace was still intact as a part-time employee.

Late one Sunday evening the phone rang. Her employer asked if she could come to work the following day. Without a second's thought, she said yes.

The next day, she woke up early and got ready. I drove her to work with her morning breakfast on her lap as we navigated Memorial Drive. I could sense her excitement to be out of the house, even for a day.

The day was short, and I picked her up from work late in the afternoon.

"How was your day?" I asked.

"Our kids were very happy petting all the animals brought in by a farm animal company," she said. The animals were all small or babies — ducks, goats, chickens, rabbits, and many more.

"Cool," I commented.

After years of isolation and a change from normal, the building where my wife works was alive with small creatures from the farm.

Minutes after we settled in at home, my wife commented, "There was one animal missing, though, during the event."

Then it occurred to me and I uttered loudly, "Possibly that was the very reason you were called in to report to the office."

We both lol over dinner.

PAPA

Ethan, eight, is an active and smart little boy from Okotoks. His exposure to his parents' knack for running a home-based business was great. Direct selling caught his interest and enthusiasm.

One weekend in the summer he asked his parents to buy him the stuff he needed for a business. His plan revolved around selling ice cream floats in front of their house.

Supplies and materials were assembled and readied for the following day. His sales weren't that bad for a beginner like Ethan.

The idea of selling stuff went beyond their front door. Global Fest, the most explosive fireworks festival in Alberta, proved enticing for the family to introduce their ice cream floats. Plans were made. On the first day of the festival, sales were dismal. They needed to improve the packaging and message of the product.

I had a talk with Tim, Ethan's dad, on how to position his product so people would notice it. Listening to our conversation, Ethan asked Tim, "Papa, why were so few people buying the floats?"

Tim responded, "It's always like this, Ethan. People aren't familiar yet with floats as a street refreshment."

"But Papa, many kids like it, right?" Ethan's first word in any conversation always starts with addressing his dad as "Papa."

I haven't counted, but my guess is that Ethan's interaction with his dad produced dozens of "Papas." This way of addressing a father is very common to Filipino-Canadians. Papa is a word of respect and authority in the household.

At times, Tim got little irritated because of Ethan's insistence that things be accomplished. To lighten their stressful moment, I asked Tim and Ethan to come to my side and said, "What makes a dad and a son so close with each other?" Both were puzzled.

At that instant, Chim, Ethan's mom, who's usually so quiet, burst into laughter when I said, "It's called 'Papa-Ethan' (a popular meat dish well loved by Filipinos)."

THANKFUL HEART

The mid-afternoon temp was high, and the Olympic Plaza was packed with people. Over fifteen food vendors' booths/trucks were scattered around. Fiesta Filipino was one of the many summer events in Calgary. Over a thousand souls braved the afternoon heat, noise, boring program, and more of the same stuff typical of any Filipino event.

It took us only a few minutes to walk and look around. Two women occupied an eight-seater metal bench under a tree. I thanked them for allowing us to occupy the vacant spots. A conversation was ignited, and our common observations and experiences established trust and ensured mutual respect.

Moments later, a young mom and her toddler came along. At first, she just watched her kid playing with other kids metres away from where we were sitting, but then she inched slowly toward the vacant spot. Without any word, she rested and smiled at us.

Our talk and interaction expanded. In no time she became an active part of our exchanges. Her kid's name was Danica, a two-year-old healthy, happy, and bubbly toddler.

Every minute or two, Danica ran to her mom for a drink or affirmation of what she was doing. The moment she was with the adults, she wasn't shy about answering questions from us. She witnessed how her mom was interacting with us. Our pleasant and joyful conversation made her trusting and at ease.

After thirty minutes of knowing each other, Danica interrupted us, asking her mom for a snack. Pop and cookies were consumed quickly, then she was back to her playtime with the other kids.

The smell of siomai (an exotic Asian cuisine) was enticing. Our bench was just twenty metres away from the food tent, and the wind was blowing in our direction. A friend of ours seated across from us indicated her craving for this food. My wife, friend, and Maricar, Danica's mom, agreed to grab some of this exotic food.

Maricar called Danica and told her to not go anywhere. I smiled at Danica and assured her that I'd be around while her mom grabbed the food. Confidently, she agreed to her mom's instruction. The plan seemed to be going well; however, minutes after the ladies had gone, Danica approached me with a fearful look.

Where's my mom?" She started running around the bench looking for her mom. I stood up, took her arm, and assured her that her mom would be back in a minute. Her anxiety became pronounced. She wanted to see her mom right there and then.

I calmly asked her to grab my pointer finger and led her in the direction where the smell of siomai was coming from. While walking in a crowded and noisy pathway, I made sure that her mom was in the crowd. "Mommy, Mommy, where are you?" I said it loud enough for her to hear.

From a distance, I saw a cop quickly glance in our direction. Danica's little hands holding my finger was a good assurance that she was secure and fine. People were staring at this old man with a little blonde toddler walking in the crowd. Moments later, I saw Maricar standing in front of the food truck. It was easy to locate her because she was wearing the same dress as Danica.

When she saw her mom, Danica released her grip on my finger. Maricar's look calmed down when I told her that Danica was anxious about her whereabouts. Her mom had taken so long because the food truck had run out of siomai stock. We were all back at our bench station in no time.

As we continued talking, Danica looked at me. Without any prompting from her mom, she said, "Thank you for finding my mom." That was a blast coming from a two-year-old kid.

That spirit and sense of thankfulness from Danica made our day. We went home with our Filipino spirit festive.

Cool.

CIRCLE OF LIFE

As planned, my workmate was out of his house the first day of September. This was one of his biggest decisions approaching his retirement. Unable to find a place in the interior of British Columbia, the couple's temporal option was to stay for a while with their daughter in Calgary. The first day was flawless, because the daughter was still on holidays. On the third day, their daughter and her boyfriend came home.

The following week, the dynamic changed. One morning my mate was early to report to the office, and he had a load of house stuff, as directed by his daughter, to store temporarily at the back of our office (bay). He mentioned that decibels inside the house were closer in between and higher. The lingering COVID health directives, and his daughter's OCD at home, made their stay seem challenging and suffocating.

The next day, my workmate arrived late and related the past night's unusual episode. They were surprised to see different coloured stickers posted in major areas of the house—shoe racks, refrigerator, drawers, closets, washroom, etc. Each couple in the house had their own colour-coded area of responsibilities.

Then he commented, "Looks like we're being directed by an invisible millennial hand. We didn't expect retirement to be this way."

I looked at his cluttered worktable and said, "Your daughter has a point."

We both lol!

ONE FOR EACH

Years back, even before the pandemic, my car was broken into. In it was one of the garage openers, taken by the thief. The garage was wide open when I woke up the following morning. Not much of value was taken, so I guessed the intruder was disappointed. One important item, though, was missing. The other garage opener.

It became a hassle for my daughter and I to park, close the garage, and make sure we didn't misplace the only opener left.

Amazon delivered a new set of garage openers weeks later. It took me days to seriously find time to reactivate the two new garage openers. The instructions were clear, but my understanding was not. First, second, and third tries didn't work. I resorted to texting my friend Jack (of all trades).

Workload, stress, or aging showed in his face, and a forced smile greeted me. His wife, though, was upbeat. I told him my dilemma. He tried the old one, read the manual, and figured it out. Twice missed. The third time, all three openers were up and running.

At dinner time, my daughter asked, "So we have three garage openers. What should we do with the old one?"

We both looked at my wife, smiling. She likes keeping and securing things for future use. However, she declined our suggestion. The old garage opener will not be part of her purse.

ONCE AGAIN

Occasionally I drove through the McDonalds on my way to work. Out of habit, I always ordered breakfast meal combo # 8.

Familiarity allowed a few moments of pleasantry with the old lady at the till.

"So your wife forgot to cook your food this morning?" she teased me.

"Nope, there was no food to cook," I responded.

VANITY?

The dictionary defines vanity as "an excessive pride in or admiration of one's own appearance or achievements." When most of the public health mandates were lifted, people scrambled to reignite their fun-filled community events. An event is usually a place to flaunt one's vanity.

In the summer of 2022, the Filipino community spared no time and initiated various events. Fashion shows, ear-piercing band concerts, movie-star-filled celebrations, cultural presentations, and the like dominated the summer landscape.

Many parents were trapped in these vanity-themed events. It brought pride to see their kid adulated and appreciated by many. At a very young age, these kids were honed, trained, and sometimes obligated to follow the whim of their parents. Catwalking, singing, dancing, and playing musical instruments would bring them to stardom. Many ventured, but more were disappointed.

Though COVID provided enough time for these aspiring stars to level up their talents, there seemed less concern about quality craftmanship and performances. It was below par in terms of presentation and content, and originality was far from present. Everything seemed to be of the same genre. Not much to desire at the end of the day.

Everything was back to normal. Trying hard vanity.

Where art thou, COVID's sting?

HE OR SHE?

Weeks away to his retirement, my workmate was busy working on some documents with Pension Canada. He was confused while trying to discern the gender of the person who had emailed him a bunch of information to consider. He wanted to know the gender of Marian so that he could communicate in the email appropriately.

We talked more, speculated, and presumed. At the end we concluded that she was a man! Just saying!

TRENDING

Watching Filipino movies on Netflix opened my mind to a new opportunity. Though over 90 per cent of the movie stars aren't known to me, I still admire their acting. One interesting observation, though, was the look, profile, and demeanour of these new movie personalities. Most of the new ones are "halfers"—half Filipino and half Caucasian. The blending was very desirable. This observation was proven by many of our friends who are married to a white spouse. Their kids are movie star calibre.

With the economic havoc wrought by the pandemic, many single immigrants and foreign workers were stuck to despair—economically and relationally. One day this topic was brought out in one of my conversations with friends. At the end of the chat, I proposed the idea to them. The reality, practicality, and viability of the idea was met with strong endorsement from them.

Settling with a Caucasian and having children from this relationship is a viable step to a bright and comfy future if they engage their young ones in TV, the arts, movies, and entertainment in the Philippines. The trend is taking off for many Filipinos married to other races around the world. I would say this is one of the consequences of staying too long in front of the TV watching Filipino movies. One could always spot an opportunity.

FIFTIETH YEAR!

It was mid-September when we watched the Calgary Opera's Fiftieth Year Gala Celebration at the Jubilee Auditorium. Our seats were four rows away from the stage, so close enough to clearly see the performers and the orchestra. That was the closest I'd been in my long years of watching events in this arts facility. Courtesy of my friend, our seating location was perfect.

Attached to the big curtain hanging on the stage was a rectangular white screen.

Moments later, the program started. A short history and accomplishments of the opera was narrated. Two alternating conductors graced the night with beautiful pieces of music. Six opera singers belted out their best voices, impressive enough for the audience to applaud with great appreciation. For every Italian and French piece, a corresponding English translation was flashed on the white screen. To fully appreciate the rendition of the opera, I had to tilt my head a bit upward.

Then came one song sung in English, and I saw the same English translation on the screen. "What's that for?" I asked my friend. The translation was for the guests in the audience who didn't speak or understand English. I just nodded at his explanation and to relax my neck from stiffening up.

The last part of the program, as expected, was a standing ovation for all the performers and orchestra players.

Back in the car, we all agreed that the show was nice, classy, and worth the time. Except two days later my neck was still sore.

ACREAGE BARN

My workmate's search for acreage somewhere in the Kelowna area yielded a negative result. He spent over two weeks looking for some with no luck.

One late Monday morning, upon his return to work, he asked me to take a look at the property he was checking out on the internet. It was in the same area but in a fringe part of the region. It was a fifteen-acre lot with a big house and lots of barns around.

He indicated his plan to build a small abode for his cousin and mom. "That's a noble and smart idea," I said. "So you'll be missing this office when you're out for your retirement." He nodded, and I followed up with, "As you're a man of all trades, you can easily build or transform one of the barns into a replica of our office."

"Nope!" he said with disdain. Then he added, "Of course, my wife wanted our room to be painted with the same colour as the one here in the office. Why couldn't I get away with the commission?" We both lol.

THE DISTANCE

One Friday evening, Aydin called. "Of course, we're available Tuesday night," was my response to his question.

Udeng was Divina's dad. He would be visiting Canada and helping with the rearing of two little boys, Tauren and Matteo. Aydin and Divina looked forward to this day when the needed help would materialize.

The Tuesday afternoon was scheduled for Udeng's welcome party, and a few guests were invited—close friends and family members, around seven adults and six children.

We arrived five minutes after my promised arrival. I felt ok because the gap of my late-coming was getting smaller.

The dining room smelled good. On the table were highly sought after Filipino dishes. My palate was whetted. Kids were running around, adults were chit chatting, and the food was getting cold. The first gesture was to locate the newcomer, Udeng. Aydin's mom, Lucia, told me to proceed to the outside deck at the back of the house.

Indeed, there were Tony, Lucia's hubby, and Udeng. Two couches in an L-shape arrangement separated the two-by-roughly-six-and-a-half feet. Between the two grandparents was nineteen-month-old Tauren.

When I looked outside, I saw Tauren not even talking or interacting with his granddads. Even so, the two guys were just trying to be civil, polite, and respectful of each other's silence.

I took the middle position on the couch, between the two guys. The usual preliminaries were said, with Tony in English and with Udeng in our dialect. The ice was broken, but it was still difficult to bring out a topic or issues common to the three of us.

My questions elicited answers from Udeng regarding his experience of travelling from the laid-back town of Pangasinan in the Philippines to his newfound place of residence. It was a shock for him, as it had been his first plane ride outside of the Philippines. The ten-hour layover in Hong Kong was too much. Another twelve hours from Hong Kong to Vancouver was punishing. I asked, "Why didn't you have any stopover in between?"

I was the language broker for Tony and Udeng.

Then it occurred to me that their distance from each other wasn't because of the virus. It was the barrier in language and dialect. I sensed that their distance and lack of speaking made them more comfortable, so I shifted my focused to Tauren, who hadn't shown any concern for people around him.

Even during dinner time, I was at the centre of Tony and Udeng's comfort zone. I suspected this was one of the reasons they wanted us to be there, to add warm bodies to the room. The pandemic distance, language barrier, importance of the occasion, and related aspect of our visit made sense.

Ha ha ha ha …

TRUTH AND RECONCILIATION

In 2021 the Government of Canada declared September 30 (my birthday) as Truth and Reconciliation Day and Orange Day for commemorating the horrific history of residential school survivors. The second year, 2022, my group, DAS, decided to remember and reflect on the injustices experienced by our Indigenous friends. Part of our reflection was this poem:

The Leaves of Fall

Red, yellow, orange leaves scattered around.
Bouncing, flipping, and dancing in the ground
Fall is here and the glorious summer behind
Change in seasons, natures purposely planned!

Step closer, pick up one, touch, feel, smell it
Maybe soft, wet, dry, crisp, cracked, or brittle

From the youth of green to its amazing colour
In a span of time the transformation complete

You tossed it upward, fell back to where it belonged
Reunited with friends, bouncing, flipping in the ground
The cool breeze, melody of the wind's soothing sound
Then it occurred to you, a memory so sad and profound

Scattered around in the meadows, plains, and parks
Unmarked graves, like the leaves resting on the grass
Stories unwritten, memories trampled and trashed
Their time has come so early and horribly so fast.

As we go out and gaze at these colourful leaves
Orange to the core, may we find peace and solace
Pause, remember those nameless young little faces!
For truth and reconciliation will put us all at peace

We were all at peace when we left the place. As we walked back to
the parking lot, I saw an Indigenous person trying to pry open the door
of my car. He retreated when I asked what he was doing.

He answered, "Is this your car?" and retreated fast.

Truth and reconciliation—a person, Indigenous or not, must know
the truth and reconcile it to himself first if the very essence of this phrase
is to be remembered and commemorated.

Truth is the main dose. Reconciliation is the booster. These are the
vaccines against the virus of hate and retaliation.

SALMON RUN

At first, we were debating whether to proceed or not. Highway 1 east of
Golden was under construction and closed to traffic. We had booked
our hotel weeks ahead, and then days before our travel an advisory was
released. From October 7 to 11, the highway would be open for the long
weekend and holiday. It was Thanksgiving Monday that weekend. Thank
goodness.

Our destination was the Adams River's Salmon Run Festival in
Shuswap, British Columbia. We left Calgary around 7:30 in the morning.

Five cars went ahead and waited for us at a Parks Canada Info Centre parking lot in Field, British Columbia. There were only four young people in the group. The remaining nineteen of us were all prone to lots of stopovers. Bladder-challenged folks.

The road approaching Golden was really in disarray. This time there was no request for another pee break. As we came closer to our destination, our excitement got intense.

In the last leg of our trip, I was asked to lead the group. Two GPSs, a written note, and memory led us exactly to the parking lot at the site. The unpaved and dusty lot was full of vehicles with different license plates. Fortunately, we parked just metres away from the exit. The reception area was littered with booths, kiosks, and other stations. The north side housed the big stage for the day's big event.

We wasted no time. We went straight and followed the flow of people. The railings on the viewing deck were covered with visitors. Moments later, we were able to squeeze into the rail. The river was shallow, and we tried hard to scan the riverbed for the famous salmon. Nope. Only splashes appeared on the surface. We scouted for more, but nothing. I looked around and saw a group of people excitedly talking to one of the guides. I waited. Once the conversation was over, I approached her.

"Hello, so tell me where to look for these beautiful creatures," I said. I was told to just follow the group to the south side of the trail down to the riverbank.

Minutes into our trek and from a distance, we saw a line of people touching the mouth of the river. That segment of the river was shallow. We got to the spot and, like the rest of the people, tried very hard to watch the salmon swimming against the flow of the river. Minutes later, I concluded that there were more people in the area than salmon. A bit frustrated, I approached another warden or guide and said, "We were told to come here to see more salmon, but it looks like there are more people than salmon around this area."

The river was still warm, and the throng of salmon were waiting for the cooler weather before they'd eventually swim upstream. I believed her explanation.

The only thing left for my friends was to take selfie. Indeed, they lined up at the riverbank and took no end of selfies. It occurred to me that they all looked like sardines in a newly opened can.

Several of my friends weren't happy. We drove almost seven hours only to watch no more than seven salmon struggling to swim upstream. I understood their frustration. It took me time to figure out how to ease the situation. Then it occurred to me. "The salmon waited for four years to swim upstream in this river to spawn then die. We, at the max, will spend no more than fifty hours experiencing and observing the salmon struggle to continue the survival of their species. The reality of the travel was insightful and significant. We still have more chances to get back and watch salmon run. However, for the salmon, they will only have one run in their lifetime."

Well said.

The drive back home was smooth and full of thanksgiving for the experience.

SINGER'S FEE

Part of our community events was a performance of a singer or dancer. One evening I came across this young man who sang well. Many testified to his talent. We had a talk, and he agreed to perform at one of our social gatherings.

Then came the moment. His attire, demeanour, and rendering of his song were awesome. Everyone was entertained and felt good. At the end of our debriefing, I asked, "So how much do we owe you for your talents?"

He answered, "$1,200.00."

After expenses, we made roughly $750.00 from our sponsors, and we owed this young man more than that. We learned our lesson. Before going into an agreement with a professional performer, though she or he may be a friend of yours, a signed contract is needed.

I felt very uncomfortable, and my board was staring at me with contempt. Why would I do that?

Then the alarm went off loudly. I woke up sweating. Phew. That was a bad dream, I guessed.

REUNION

For a while, the list of names was for our high school room section only. Then as the excitement went viral, all the other classmates were included. At last count, we had over two hundred people, including other classmates from our high school days. The goal was to reach out to all and have our next year's grand school reunion sometime in 2025.

The organizers pressured me to say yes. I haven't booked my travel, but I'm positively considering the idea. Besides, my wife and I will then be retired. Time and opportunity abound.

I followed the messenger chat every day and was happy to see names and connect them to a face and mannerism. Reminiscing about the past with these people through social media was a stress reliever.

One early morning, though, the roll was getting long. Then one comment came out. It was saddening. Fourteen of our classmates were gone. This reinforced my desire to visit and join the reunion.

THE CRUISE THAT WAS

Our children booked our Hawaiian cruise months before our fortieth anniversary. The treat coincided with my wife's December 2021 retirement and my sixty-fifth birthday.

As planned, our flight, taxi, hotel check-in, and cruise boarding went well. My daughter's worry eased when I assured her that we still have the stamina and mind to face the challenges and hassles of our fifteen-day trip.

The relatively lesser traffic at the YYC airport afforded us an easy arrival at the departure gate. We settled there for over an hour, boarded, and then the plane took off shortly. Cookies and pretzels came for the snack. The landing was smooth.

The ride from the airport to the Best Western on Davie Street was hassle-free. The taxi driver was friendly, and we heard an abridged version of his fourteen years in Canada. Very interesting.

As we got out of the taxi, we saw tables in the south side driveway of the hotel. The sound of music was loud. Bottles of drinks on the table were empty and many. The people enjoying their time together stared at us with curiosity. We stared back at them with forced smiles. The chubby young guy behind the counter gave us the same forced smile when we approached him. A few clicks on his keyboard and he handed me two door cards and two complimentary breakfast tickets.

Early the following morning, rested and ready, we proceeded to the hotel's restaurant. Our orders came ten minutes later. The omelette, other side offerings, and a coffee made the difference. We felt fueled and energized.

We walked out the sliding door of the hotel, and in front of us was this taxi driver who seemed to be patiently waiting for us. He opened his cab trunk and handily arranged our luggage inside. He thought we were going back home from a trip, but we told him to just proceed to Canada Place. Minutes later, he drove us down the belly of the building, and there we found hundreds of people lining up to board the ship.

We didn't wait for the scheduled two o'clock boarding time. Confidently, we followed the flow of our fellow travellers to the gates swarmed with cruise personnel. When we reached the final screening point, the lady behind the stand handed us two small plastic packages, as if we were Olympic winners. Two medallions with our names etched on them would be our access device into the ship.

We saw another line of people when we entered the Muster Point located on the seventh deck. Final confirmation of our identity was complete, and the agent in front of us looked at the gadget he was holding and compared our tired and stressed faces with our photos on his computer screen. The resemblance was there, so we were welcomed with a sigh. Moments later, we wandered around and located our assigned stateroom. As expected, the Filipino attendants were very helpful. Three floors up, left turn, and another turn to the right landed us at our cage, C424.

We spent no time unpacking our carry-on bags and checking in our luggage. Our first exploration of the ship yielded exactly what we were looking for. First on our list was the buffet restaurant, Lido, on the fifteenth deck. When the elevator opened, our nostrils enjoyed a fiesta feeling. The heavy breakfast I'd had at the hotel seemed to be gone.

As we entered the hall, we were greeted with the strong smell of food. Long lines of people again. Almost all the tables were taken. The tables close to the window overlooking the port of Vancouver were fully occupied. We slowly approached the buffet and grabbed the food we knew wasn't good for our health. I rationalized that my maintenance pills would save me from the consequences of my unhealthy cravings for fifteen days. One thing I was thankful for—the breakfast offerings were different from my everyday bowl of oatmeal at home.

Our plates were full. Bacon was placed on top of the other gastronomic items. The coffee was great. Orange juice on the side and polite, friendly attendants on hand made our meal comfortable. Before we started to dig in, my wife remembered one important promise to our daughter. The small rubber animals—bear, sheep, praying mantis, and walrus—we'd brought with us had to be part of our photo ops in and around the ship. We placed them together in between our plates. People were staring not at us but at these creatures. I responded to one comment with, "These are our portable pets." Right away I sent the pic to my daughter. Her joy that day was overwhelming. The walrus was her representation. The bear was her brother. The sheep was my wife, and I was the praying mantis.

As we enjoyed our food and took note of most people lining up in the hallway, we observed that this cruise was designed for and catered to gray-haired people. Hearing aids were visible and protruding from the ears of several guests; walking canes moved in sync with the slow-paced steps created by uneven shoe heels and manifested in swaying hips; hanging eyeglasses rested just halfway down the nostril; some oversized mid-sections; postures that seemed looking for lost coins on the floor; well-kept, thinning gray hair, or the lack of it; and wrinkles like the ocean's waves mirrored in most of the faces. Over 50 per cent, by my educated estimate, of the guests walked like wobbly, stooping penguins.

The glitters hanging in the ears and on the necks and wrists of the women were obviously displayed. I couldn't believe we were part of this floating community. But truth settled in. We were part of this oldies floating city.

Our first meal was satisfying. We decided to explore the ship some more. Each station we stopped by was manned mostly by Filipinos, so there was no difficulty in our conversation. The guy in Fantasy Lounge was from the Bicol area. He wanted us to book a day of relaxation for only $20 US. I looked at my wife, and in less than a second, we communicated our thoughts and came up with a solid no. We didn't say it out loud to him, but our body language said it all. He got the cue.

The walkway around the ship would take 2.8 rounds for a two-mile walk. I hated converting kilometres to miles. It altered my calculating mind to numerically challenged territory.

It was my nap time when we got back to our nest. The medallions we were wearing amazed us. Every time we stopped in front of the digital info panel, our names appeared with a caption, "Happy Anniversary Romeo and Nida." And every time we reached our door, just less than a metre away, it automatically unlocked. The medallions even made ordering a drink faster. A tap on the gadget did it all. I asked one of the attendants about it, and he pointed to a white, bowl-size disk attached at the sealing panel. I was told it was like a drone that monitored and tracked guests on the ship. So our whereabouts every day was being recorded and logged in. The type of drinks we ordered and the places we'd been to. Every day.

The next day we tried to book our formal day reservation at the Da Vinci Restaurant. After the third try, I didn't hesitate to ask for help from one of the staff. He spoke Filipino, which gave me confidence, but he wasn't able to book us. Our time was short, and we needed to book. It created an unpleasant moment with my wife. She insisted that I should have done the booking on the first day of our trip. I tried my best to find ways to make our formal night possible. A walk to one of the lounges was a blessing in disguise. The personnel manning the photo centre asked how he could help. I told him our predicament, and with a few strokes our booking for the formal night was confirmed.

We were ready in our best attire for the event one hour ahead of schedule. While we were in the line, the smiling receptionist greeted us enthusiastically. After checking our medallions, we were led to one of the corners of the restaurant. Moments later, all the tables around us were occupied. We smiled back at the Asian couple sitting next to our table. The grandeur of the room was noticeable, with fresh flowers on each table. People started "selfieing," including us, of course.

Kim approached us with two copies of the menu. I asked him what dish he would recommend. I ordered halibut and duck for my wife.

"Masarap po ang order ninyo," said Kim.

After minutes of waiting, I enjoyed my order, but my wife wasn't happy. The smell, preparation, and presentation of her order were great. However, it took her extra time and effort to chew the rubbery duck meat. It didn't meet her expectation.

Our time at the restaurant was great except for the duck. We came out with my wife squawking inaudibly. Our steps were wobbly because of the wine we'd ordered. It made no difference, we thought, because most of the guests behind and in front of us walked like us too.

Our next destination was the Champaign Falls event at the Piazza, the main lobby of the ship. Hundreds of champaign cups were arranged like a pyramid, and steps were placed close to the table stand of the Champaign Falls. Over thirty bottles were opened for participating guests to pour over from the top of the champaign bottle pyramid. We didn't pass up this opportunity.

As we stepped aside from the crowd, we saw a thumbs up from one of the Filipino supervisors roaming around. He came from his station to approach us. He was from one of the islands in the Visaya region of the Philippines. He talked and we listened. Another story to remember. He led us to one of the empty tables. One of the servers, this time a Filipina, took our orders. Mojito for my wife and Corona for me. That was a refreshing and interesting night. From champaign, mojito, to beer—all in one night's experience.

At midnight our bed started to shift right, left, forward, and backward. The following morning was the nightmare of many. Though this was our second time in a cruise ship, we heard many guests in the dining room talking about the rough seas. Indeed, I was one of the many. Seasickness or motion sickness was the topic. I was reminded of my childhood experience with an earthquake in the Philippines many decades ago. My balance, appetite, and composure were compromised. Throwing up would be a shameful act, so I just sucked it up. Our plan to go around and explore the other places on the ship was cancelled. The power of the mind became powerless. My wife and I just had a very small breakfast. The amount, variety, and invitation of the food weren't our priority anymore. We had to finish our food fast and ask around for where to get relief.

We were about to finish our last bite when another guest asked if he could join us at the table. Pasquali introduced himself as an Italian gynecologist, eighty-five years old, from Victoria Island. His wife was still in the bed. Barely five feet tall, Pasquali possessed vitality and energy. In just a few exchanges, we were able to connect and established a good vibe. It was his (and his family's) thirty-fifth cruise. We were impressed, but no amount of impression could mitigate my nausea. Halfway through his plate, he jokingly offered me a bargain. Out of nowhere with a cunning smile, he wanted to trade four cows for my wife. I took the bait and played his game. He declined my counteroffer. The deal could have been done if he had four and a half cows to trade.

My wife asked his secret of a long life. He prescribed a daily dose of laughter, wine, finding new friends, and lots of sex with his spouse.

The swaying and swerving of the *Princess* compelled me to ask his opinion of why this was happening. We had to go to the guest services desk. At the same time, he assured us that once the ship passed the strait along the coast of Oregon, everything would be back to normal.

The guest services staff pointed us to the small boutique across the aisle. The lady behind the till directed us to a corner where the Dramamine, Gravol, and other medications were hanging. I really needed to cure my seasickness to enjoy our days on the sea. I had a second look at the pills. The third time around, miraculously, my nausea faded slowly. My wife was surprised. The healing was psychological. It was the price.

Pasquali was right. The following morning was smooth sailing.

On the fourth day we were early in the buffet line. We looked around for Pasquali. We guessed he slept in. The food trays were the same as the days before. We grabbed items we seldom cook at home, and many of them. We were getting accustomed to the greetings of the servers. Once settled at our table, a server would ask us about drinks.

Our answers were always the same—black coffee, water, and orange juice. We just copied most of the other guests' orders. Our connection with the servers was instant and great. Their greetings always started with, "Good morning, Po."

"Po" was the spark that brighten our days.

After our "brunch," we proceeded to deck seven of the ship. The perfume boutique store was our destination. My wife had forgotten to bring her favourite perfume, and I took pride and indicated my plan to grab one for her. She just sighed. We strolled around the store and scouted for the cheapest item. When we went out of the door, I whispered, "With all the samples you tried, I guessed you don't need one." The brand items on display were limited, and the prices were horrendously high and in US dollars. After the trip, we agreed to visit Costco or The Bay for a better buy. Off we went from the store, smiling, and the saleslady followed us with a strange stare.

The next day we decided to buy gift items at a store that sold t-shirts, hats, etc. I let my wife do the buying, and she was so thankful. We brought cash, as using our credit card wasn't an option. We'd had a bad experience during our first cruise to the Caribbean many years back when our credit card was hacked. This time we just wanted to pay with cash. The saleslady gave us the receipt and directed us to pay for the items at the guest services desk. I handed the hundred-dollar bill to the Latina behind the desk. "Gracias!" She grabbed it and took a marker from the drawer. She swiped it briefly. I asked what that was for, and she explained that it was their way of making sure the money wasn't fake. We got it. Minutes later, she gave me the receipt and the change in bills. Before we stepped out of her sight, I asked her if she could swipe the change with the marker—to make sure we weren't receiving a fake dollar bill in return. She complied. We all lol.

Our first day of the land tour was frantic. The couple in front of us in line were from Oregon. A smile and "How are you, sir?" started our conversation. They'd flown from Oregon to Vancouver for this trip. It was the couple's tenth cruise. I politely manoeuvred our talk to their country's politics. Both said their present political theatre was a joke.

Their president was a shame to the country and abroad. I was aware of this. It was no secret.

As a retired US Navy officer, the guy was proud to share his story. His deployment to various naval stations around the country was memorable. We listened curiously. After his piece, I related my dad's desire for me to become a member of the US Navy. After my high school graduation, my dad took me to Subic Naval Base in Zambales, Philippines. The Navy recruitment then was open. As a member in the US Army himself, my dad wanted me to follow in his footsteps with the US armed forces. The Navy was the opportunity before me.

One day before the exam and screening, my dad brought me to the barber shop. My long hair that I'd cherished for so long was cut down to one-tenth of an inch. Only a small patch on top of my head was left. I really looked like a fresh recruit. To make the long story short, I didn't make the cut. We went home sad. The next time I met my friends I told them I was a "US Never." This story made the couple laughed out loud, and the people around us noticed. From outside the terminal, we saw our parked bus. Moments later, we got on the coach.

Ken was our first tour guide driver from the Polynesian Tour Bus company. He was funny and knowledgeable of the history of Hawaii. Halfway to our destination, he suggested that visiting the Arizona Memorial wasn't a good idea. For over four months, he said, the waiting time for the ferry had been four hours. Our stay in the harbour would only be an hour and a half. The suggestion was reasonable. We were told also to just bring our camera and purse with us. A carry-on bag would cost $6.00. Our bus was secured, so we left behind our bags.

In just under one hour, we reached Pearl Harbor. From a distance we secretly followed the US Navy guy and his wife. They would be our guide to the place and going back to the bus afterwards. The sun was up and shining hot. The breeze was refreshing, yet the humidity forced our skin to sweat. We strolled around and took pictures of the scenery. Moments later, we felt hungry and thirsty.

The snack store was full of people. Inflation was also a reality on the island. Our snack budget was enough to buy one big bottled water and two small bags of chips. Across from us was the gift and bookstore.

Four postcards and small items were good enough, we thought. From the corner of my eye, I saw the couple walking back to the gate. We followed them. I looked at my watch and saw that we had twenty more minutes to boarding time. As we passed the security gate, we saw other guests trailing us.

We left Pearl Harbor and drove to the famous Nu'uanu Pali Lookout. The weather was good at eighteen degrees; however, Ken warned us about the wind. He was right. We braced ourselves from the force of the howling winds and enjoyed the scenery.

The drive back to the ship was incident-free. Our rest was enough for our next trip to Luau mid-afternoon of the same day. It was one of the most sought-after excursions on the island, forty-five minutes from the pier. As we got off the bus, the receptionists pointed us to a platform. Camera ready, the photographer helped us to strike the perfect pose and positioning. Two shots done and off we trekked to the reception area in front of the stage, with two complimentary drink tickets.

We occupied the table close to the stage, and people started to fill the vacant tables scattered around. The welcome music in the air was inviting. Metres away were the splashing waves of the ocean. The line of people leading to the bar was getting long, and guests settled back at their tables when the host made the announcement. Everyone walked around the area where two staff in their native attire opened a pit. They then lifted a mesh wire with the roasted pig in it.

Back at our table, the host gave directions on how to get our food. Procedure wise, it was very organized and planned. Poi was the food buzz word of the night, a native dish that was very islandic in nature. We didn't try it.

The host made the introductions, and for over an hour we were entertained with dances, songs, and laughter.

Back at our bus, everyone said they'd had a wonderful time. Halfway to our ship, I recalled one of the very important reminders from our driver, Wendel, from Ilocos Sur. We needed to remember the numbers one and twenty-seven. Our bus number was one, and the distance from Luau to the ship was twenty-seven miles. To miss number one meant walking twenty-seven miles.

The next morning, breakfast was special. We braved to sit with two seniors sitting close to the window. Gherard, eighty-seven, and Heidi, eighty-three, from Kelowna responded well to our greetings. Our time with them covered many areas of mutual interest. We worried not about our food. We could always go back for seconds. The thing that got their attention was the reason for our cruising. Intently they listened to my story. Our children had surprised us with this trip to celebrate our fortieth wedding anniversary, the retirement of my wife last December, and my sixty-fifth b-day. Good for us, they commented. However, there was one big problem. They inched their heads closer to hear me out. All of us laughed out loud when I told them that I hadn't seen my credit card yet. My daughter borrowed it months before our trip.

The story cemented our friendship. The couple started to share their stories, including their observations on other travellers on board. They were so disgusted with the guy who spit out on the floor the food he'd tried. People who didn't close their mouths while chewing unnerved them. The unmodulated loud conversation and chatter was another annoyance. A mom with her toddler were slowly walking and looking for a table. The couple wondered if there would be a chair big enough to hold the lady's butt. We promised the couple to meet again once we were back from our next island stop, Maui, the next day.

The ship docked early in the morning, and the line was long when we reached the end of the terminal. Security was visibly present at each pier gate. Other guests waited for taxis and other forms of public transit. My wife and I decided to follow other vacationers threading a narrow pathway snaking around the pier. At the clearing, from a distance across the street, we saw the sign "Maui Mall." My wife's face brightened. Sadly, though, neither Walmart nor a Dollar Store were in the area. The mall was far smaller than the one we used to go in Calgary. It was twenty-five degrees out and our sweat compelled us to take cover under the shade of the plant dome in the middle of the mall. I let my wife roam around after few minutes of rest. Our time in the island, six hours, was enough to explore the other establishments. We headed north and, presto, saw a Ross store less than a hundred metres away.

Indeed, we saw familiar faces inside. Two guys, servers, from the Da Vinci Restaurant, were happy with the items they'd bought. We exchanged smiles and greetings. We left Ross with our legs begging for a rest.

The table in a rest area inside the mall was occupied by a lone guy. He said we could use the other chairs in front of him. I initiated the conversation, and in less than thirty minutes, we learned so much about him. He was a retired detective from the Maui police force and was married to a Filipina from Ilocos Sur. Adobo was one of his favourite Filipino dishes. He had never been to the Philippines but often travelled to Hong Kong. His private investigation company kept him busy. He was constantly looking at his watch. We looked at the time too, ensuring time to walk back to the ship after a few minutes of chit chat.

We were ahead of the line when we reached the gate manned by two custom or pier security personnel. I supposed they were still following a strict COVID policy. Oversized hats, sunglasses, and masks covered all the skin on their faces. If not for the accent of the older one, I wouldn't have figured out their race. Both were natives of Ilocos, again. One stared at my passport and looked at me. I sensed her smile behind the mask. I said, "Salamat po (Thank you)." She said, "Salamat din po (Thank you too)."

The air conditioning system of the ship was great. We were relieved when we reached our room. After putting away our stuff, we proceeded to the food area. Indeed, we were hungry. Gherard and Heidi were seated in one corner. With trays of food in our hands, we joined them. The fun started. Heidi swore that, so far, this was their most fun trip because of our presence and friendship with them. I ate more to fill my ego. Our over one hour of talk ended when Heidi and I yawned at the same time. Nap time for all of us.

Early the following day, we were once again in the line for our next excursion. The destination was the famous Akaka Falls and the Macadamia Nut Shop in Hilo. Our driver this time was Nestor. He whispered to us that the price of macadamia products was way cheaper in Walmart. Noted.

The narrow and winding road was like the one highway leading to the summer capital of the Philippines—Baguio.

The 442-foot Akaka Falls was one of the most visited tourist attractions on the island. It took us over half an hour to navigate the 0.4-mile paved loop. The Akaka Falls provided stunning scenery, but we noted the absence of any birds or animals in the area. Intriguing. We neither heard nor saw any wild animals in or around the vicinity.

The highway leading to the next stop was winding and narrow. In less than thirty minutes, we reached one of the tourist attractions on the Island—Panaewa Rainforest Zoo and Gardens. This twelve-acre zoo housed over eighty species of animals, and it's the only one in the United States located in a rainforest.

As soon as we were out of the bus, we heard birds and other animal noises. From one of the bird cages, just at the back of the store's entrance, we were greeted by a parrot's "Hello." More caged animals stared at us as we stared back at them in civility. Llamas, anteaters, salamanders, colourful birds, parrots, and the like lightened our day. Though our time was limited, we were fascinated by the creatures in cages.

As our bus exited the zoo onto the main highway, one observation occurred to me. I wondered if all the animals in Akaka Falls had been captured and transported to the zoo. That remained to be seen, I thought.

After several turns and stops, we got off the bus and headed to one of the island's tourist stores. My wife pulled out the list of candies, cookies, and macadamia-related products she wanted to buy. Again, Nestor whispered and advised us to just go to Walmart for a bargain price. That was a good and practical idea, we thought, so we entered the store out of curiosity and to buy limited gift items. It just so happened that our driver was ahead of us at the till. The lady behind the counter knew him. He was even given a discount. My observation was right. The stopover at the store was part of his company's incentives for their driving crew.

We left the store with two plastic bags full of stuff, and a couple of hundred US dollars poorer. Part of the pier's security protocols was to inspect our stuff going into the pier terminal. I placed my backpack on the belt for X-ray inspection. When it got off the black compartment, the lady motioned to the other security officer to check on the bag. I heard her say that she'd seen some rocks at the bottom of the bag. Obligingly, I opened and emptied my bag. People around me heard the lady, and others simply stopped and waited for the next episode.

"There were rocks inside your bag," said the security guy.

I showed the small black bag to him. Slowly, I unzipped it and, presto, our portable pets (walrus, bear, sheep, and preying mantis) were on display before him and the rest of the people around me. We all laughed out loud.

Our last anchorage was in Kona the following morning. We kept in our mind the Filipino driver's advice. The cruise agent gave us a map on which we could follow the route to Walmart. A fifteen-to-twenty-minute uphill walk was no big deal. I still remembered our K-country eighteen-kilometre trail walk. This one was peanuts, we thought.

As the sliding door of the store opened, we felt at home right away. To the right was McDonald's. We resisted the call. More free, better, and tasty food selections were in the ship.

After a few rounds we found the shelves where our objectives were stacked up. Macadamia-based products were smiling at us. We smiled back. Moments later, we were at the till. Our basket-load was priced way lower than the one we'd had the other day. Then we worried if we had space in our luggage for this stuff. We were the only ones walking back to our ship along a wide and long highway down the hill. Fortunately, we reached the coffee and gift shop just minutes before the rain poured.

We got into the ship just in time for our dinner. Two vacant chairs in front of two seniors caught our attention. They smiled and invited us to join them. Best of friends, the two seniors from Newfoundland were enjoying their sixth cruise. The one with more hair to keep asked what our next item on our bucket list would be. From the back of my mind and based on reality, I blurted, "Start saving for another three years for the next cruise." We all departed from each other fully fed, delighted, and in good spirits.

One early evening into our twelfth day of our voyage, the captain made an announcement. Two passengers needed emergency medical attention. Vancouver Island was the closest and most logical stopover. The news went viral. Faster than the speed of social media, one crew member answered my question the next morning. While handing out my coffee and juice, he explained that one elderly passenger broke his leg, and the other one had died of cancer. I had initially guessed it was due to a COVID infection. Of over three thousand souls on board the ship, no case of the virus was reported.

Our weeks of worry before our cruise departure circled back when the ship finally docked at Canada Place in Vancouver. We'd worried too much about COVID infections. We imagined the ship as a floating petri dish for the virus, with the most vulnerable group of people. But it was a relief.

Our cruise went well. It was non-eventful, worth the time, and insightful. We had no regrets.

CRUISE TIDBITS
Time Well Spent

One of the activities we enjoyed during the first few days of the cruise was walking around the ship. It took over ten minutes each round, and two rounds was just over one mile. Each time we passed the side window of the restaurants, we saw people inside huddling around the table. Each of the patrons had a drink on the table. Exactly as expected, their talk never ended. It was the same people after two rounds. The passing of their time was like a ritual to be cherished and respected. It was their time to seriously talk about life at the end of the run, it seemed.

The outside lounge chairs were also occupied. Some enjoyed their hard-bound books, while other were content with their little gadget. My wife and I talked about some of our observations since the start of our journey. We even projected and imagined ourselves inside those windows with other elderlies. What a time to spend with whom, where, and when. Could this be the best way to pass time?

After four rounds we went into one door. The door of the restaurant at the right was inviting. We took the corner table and waited for the server to approach us. My wife ordered Mojito and Corona Light for me.

The sweat lost was replenished in just a few minutes. We finished our drinks and walked out of the place. The pictures hanging in the photo panels were swarmed by other guests. We finally located our sample photo. Five copies of the same photo would cost us around $100.00. The price was high enough to heal my nausea.

We spent half of our day walking, looking around the windows, talking, contemplating, resting, drinking, nauseating, and mood-less to spend that money—we saw it as prelude to our later years.

Would this be the picture of time well spent?

Opportunity

Ferdinand was in charge of our suite. A high school grad many years back, he was determined to make his kids advance in life through education. His sacrifice of working for many years in the ship was obvious. I took the liberty to interview him. We found out that one of his children stopped her law schooling at the University of the Philippines due to COVID and related restrictions. He asked what opportunities were available for his daughter in Canada.

We informed him of all the possible ways for his eldest to come to Canada. The best route would be for his daughter to apply as an international student. We saw a glimmer of hope in his eyes while listening to our sharing. I told him to contact me if he had the time. He looked at the card I gave him and said, "Yes, I will give you a call after I talk to my family in the Philippines."

Our conversation ended with a little request. I needed an extension cord to plug in our gadgets. Moments later, he handed me a fifty-foot orange extension cord. Every day our gadgets were charged, and every day since then, I've waited for his call about the opportunity I presented to him.

Indeed, opportunity knocks only once.

Lotion

One early morning, fresh from the shower and with lotion sticking moistly on our skin, we hopped into the elevator. Our usual destination was Lido, the buffet kingdom. We were met with a warm welcome and smiles from the people inside the moving cubicle.

When we reached the deck, we heard murmuring behind us about the scent they'd just smelled. My wife and I neither offended nor pleased. My wife blushed and felt uncomfortable on our way to the buffet line.

We grabbed our food and settled in one corner of the hall. We talked about the incident. We both smiled upon realizing and rationalizing the reality of what had happened in the elevator. Our lotion out-scented the very common and usual smell of seniors.

Porta Pets

Our friendship with Gherard and Heidi went comfortably on. As we enjoyed our breakfast one bright, sunny day, we talked about travel, gardens, and careers. We shared several common points of interest. Mine was vegetables; Gherard's was his orchard.

Out of nowhere, I remembered our companion pets. We proudly brought them out from the small black bag. I placed them around my plate and proudly introduced them to Gherard and Heidi as our ever faithful, loyal, maintenance-free, no-feeding-required, mask-free, and COVID-free porta pests.

All the other seniors around us stared and smiled at our porta pets.

Credit Card

During our first three days of roaming around the ship, I mastered one approach to make friends. After introductions and preliminaries, I made sure to share our experience. All ears were on me when they heard my daughter had booked and paid for our cruise. As a token of her appreciation and for the celebration of our fortieth wedding anniversary, this trip was made possible.

Praise and amazement came out of their mouths.

There was only one big problem. All ears again. "I haven't seen my credit card at home for months."

All started laughing ballistically.

Living Demo

During one late-afternoon dinner, a Filipino couple asked, "So is your daughter is still living with you?"

"Yes!" I said.

This wasn't a common arrangement in Caucasian families. I indicated to our friend that we weren't worried. In fact, I informed them that my daughter's situation, being alone at home, was best for her. We were letting her experience and enjoy the special offer of seventeen-day, parent-free living.

Their daughter, twenty-seven years old, was sitting close to them, and the rest of us nodded approvingly and lol.

Accuracy?

Wendel, one of our drivers, always told us exactly when we had to get back to our bus after our tour. It gave us good sense of how long we could be at the area. There were no problems encountered.

Nestor, another driver, would tell us exactly the amount of time we'd be staying at our destination while the bus was around a hundred metres away. Seniors were hurried up and had less time to enjoy the place.

I liked Nestor's driving but preferred Wendel's timing.

The Winner Is …

The last night at the Princess Theater was a blast. All the seats were taken, and each guest had their gadget for picking the winner. *The Voice* in the ocean featured nine talents: seven men and two women. All the singers belted out their best performance. The three judges' resumes were impressive. They knew why they were there, we supposed.

The final leg of the competition was the audience participation. We had to click our gadget for the contestant we picked. I cheated three times by pressing the key three times. I was told that only one click was enough, though, after the event.

The crowd was ecstatic when the winner was announced. Second place went to one of the lady contestants. A replica of *The Voice* trophy was handed to the winner, who was the other lady. Amazingly, both were Filipinas.

My voice went up to the roof, and I saw people take off their masks to express their jubilation. The night was very memorable for us. Filipinos' singing talent was phenomenal on land and on the sea. There were so many inspirational moments on the cruise. The head chef was a Filipino, the human resources department was headed by another Filipina, and over 50 per cent of the crew was from the Philippines.

We exited the theatre with our head held up with pride. However, when we heard a loud cough behind us, we stooped and pretended to be wiping off some stuff on our faces. Then at the lobby, we greeted the winners. People were wondering what we were saying in our native tongue. Our joy infected many. The virus of appreciation was transmitted to the crowd that night.

DIABETIC NURSE

Two weeks after we arrived home from our vacation, I received a call from my doctor's office, telling me I'd be receiving a call the next day from my new "diabetic" nurse.

Indeed, per scheduled time, my phone rang. She introduced herself. Princess was the nurse who had monitored me for years, but she'd been assigned to a new post. Janis (not her real name) was my new online nurse.

After a few minutes of introduction, I quipped, "Welcome to the club!"

"What do you mean?"

"Yesterday I was informed that my new diabetic nurse would call, so I assumed you're also diabetic."

I heard her lol!

WORLD PEACE

In mid-November, a close friend of mine invited me to attend an event in one of the mosques in Calgary. The theme was so relevant, considering the world situation.

We were the first to enter the big hall. I estimated over three hundred people were there. We comfortably sat in the second row from the front. At the presenters' table were the names of invited guests, leaders representing Hinduism, Sikhism, Buddhism, Judaism, Christianity, and Islam.

The theme of the gathering was World Peace. The moderator greeted and welcomed everyone. Political and community leaders in the crowd were acknowledged. I looked behind me and saw that the hall was full. There were people of colour and several people wearing various types of head coverings or hats.

Each presenter shared their religious view and teachings on world peace, and how their founders and followers acted on the issue, as well as a summary of their faith's tenets. The moderator emphasized the need to understand and practise the common threads to achieve peace. Different thoughts, teachings, and ideals intersected and affirmed the importance of personal awareness, relationship with fellow humans and the environment, and ultimately with God.

None of the presentations received applause of appreciation or needed clarification. No questions were asked. We all looked like muted mutants. Only the digital clock hanging behind the panelists was noticeably moving.

After the session officially ended, the crowd's chatter finally got louder. One announcement caught our attention. We followed the lineup to another hall. In the middle of the room were two long tables brimming with food. While waiting for the line to move forward, my friend asked, "What struck you the most in the presentations?"

Without any hesitation, and in all seriousness, I responded, "Food is the very first step to peace." A well-nourished spirit and body are predictively the precursor of peace. We looked around and noticed, indeed, that people were happy, disciplined, and smiling at each other. A few people wore masks, but certainly their smiling eyes were visible.

We drove home at peace with ourselves and with each other.

Shalom!

RETIREMENT 1.0

My workmate officially retired on November 18, 2022. After over thirty years of service, he decided to pursue another career. Three houses were waiting for his skill in renovations and fixing things. First on the list was his mom's house in Surrey. It had a never-ending list of items to fix. Her daughter's condo in Calgary was begging for new paint and tiles. His son's condo was last on the list. Scouting for a place to move into was stalled. No doubt this one could be subjected to some modifications, based on the style and taste of his wife.

Gone were the days my mate and I talked about life, work, and hobbies. My morning normalities were altered. Just the keyboard, screen monitor, and I interacted with each other. This much time for self reflection and contemplation was overwhelming. The phone ringing was no longer a welcome melody. I preferred in person chats, but phone calls were disruptive.

One very important thing was missing. Since his departure from the office, I've run out of material to share in this book. We had a nice way of twisting, muzzling, and making up the storylines of our experiences.

I branded him as "MacGyver." Over the years we worked together, no less than five projects were started—mechanical, technical, and house related improvements. He left the office with his beast (big truck) fully loaded with clutter.

I missed his initiative and his cluttered drawers and workspace at the back room of our office bay.

RETIREMENT 2.0

The most common question my friends asked me after my retirement was, "What will you do with your time?" Before contemplating my departure from the workplace, I planned and intended to pursue my writing, travel to museums, and delve into the arts, namely photography, drawing, and resin molding.

Writing and photography were handy. I have what it takes to improve those routes. The art part was full of research and exploration. Google helped me a lot. Even my daughter gave me pointers to consider. At her workplace in the university, they've done resin mold art for years. I saw, touched, and was amazed by the sample she gave me. This strengthened my resolve to pursue the endeavour. The items, of course, would be the various Canadian grains stored in our office. The question remains, though: Would I be charged with conflict of interest for using grains as a medium of my artwork?

Well, I guess this one is a reasonable project to keep me sane and away from mental health issues now that I was alone in the workplace.

A good aspect of the pandemic. My interest in other form of self expression, like the arts, was cultivated.

RETIREMENT 3.0

Now that I was working alone, many of my friends were puzzled as to what my routine was. I told them that I'd found a way to keep myself busy and occupied.

I brought out the laptop that was assigned to us, which I seldom used. I placed it on the right end corner of my long worktable. In between was my personal laptop. The desktop computer was on the left end corner. The laptop was used for my constant contact with my supervisor in Weyburn, Saskatchewan. With our Work Team Apps, we visually talk and share the day's situation. I always made sure the laptop was on.

I used my personal laptop as a news source and for outside-the-office activities. This was my connection to people and my community. The tabletop computer was for my official duties, and it logged off every ten minutes of no activity, giving me no choice but to log in my eighteen-character password.

When work came in, I'd move the two laptops to the very end corner of the table. When news was new, I'd fold down the top half of the other laptop so I wouldn't be distracted from reading. I even had an unpleasant talk with some of the newscasters or columnists. I wasn't worried. No one was with me, and I could always raise my voice to express my opinion. When I'd hear a ding from the other laptop, I'd do the same with the other one. That was the routine of my days in front of the workstation.

There was also a limit to my routine. Boredom was a strong companion. When I felt its presence on me, I had to walk to the front receiving room of the office, where my loyal friends and confidants were comfortably resting and watching all kinds of movement outside the window. I made sure my indoor plants had enough water intake and that the window blinds were open. I even brought out the scissors to trim them. Cutting old and dying leaves had a therapeutic effect on me. Aside from making the plant look healthy and good, the sheer act of separating the unpleasant old and dying leaves was time well spent.

After this weekly occurrence, I had to go back to the back room of the office. My next routine was to dispose of the grain samples in the storage racks. There were many of these, and we were running out of empty plastic buckets. This task took care of my body movement. Thirty minutes of this produced a good amount of sweat.

Then came the phone ringing. The call sometimes ranged from five to forty-five minutes. On average, I'd talk for five minutes with the clients, less than five minutes with my family members, and not over ten minutes with friends and others.

The usual people who entered our door were the courier, mailman, and cleaner. Our short talks lasted five minutes on average. The cleaner had to do lots of wiping around, so we spent a good ten minutes talking per day.

The pandemic had its way of rearranging our daily routine.

RETIREMENT 4.0

What came to our mind one Saturday morning was downsizing. The value of our place was enough to buy a new condo, way smaller and manageable for seniors like us. The next question was the market appraisal. How much would a buyer pay for this property within the city centre boundary? We made lots of estimate and guesses based on the city's latest appraised value.

Amid our talk, an idea clicked out of my head. "I think we need to add around 5 per cent over the price of the house if we ever sell it," I said. My wife wanted to know the basis of this assertion. We'd been occupying the house for over twenty-five years. During that span of time, my wife had collected lots of gifts, memorabilia, and tangible memories from different people and places, like the Dollar Store, Walmart, and "VV Boutique" (Value Village). The appraised value of this stuff loitering around the house, on the main floor and downstairs, would cost, in my closest estimate, over 5 per cent of the house price.

My wife stared at me for a second and we both lol. "Agreed!" she said.

Phew ...

RETIREMENT 5.0

When my wife retired in December 2021, my family planned what to do with our basement. The place would be an ideal rent space for students, whether international or from the university. The latter one was an easy sell. My daughter was working at the university, so she was aware of the great need for student housing.

The fact that we haven't touched or moved anything yet means that the basement looks like an organized junkyard.

Out of nowhere when the issue was brought up, I said, "I think we need to buy a portable GPS and a high-powered flashlight in a glass case, installed on the wall leading downstairs." My wife didn't get it right away.

Any student who wanted to check out the basement would use the GPS to navigate the terrain, and the flashlight to make the terrain visible.

"Good one, Dad!" said my daughter. My wife just smirked.

RETIREMENT 6.0

I phoned Greg one afternoon. With regret, he couldn't attend our Christmas party, as he was committed to another event that day. Our talk shifted to my retirement.

He asked, "So what are you going to do in your retirement?"

I told him that I'd possibly be extending my stay for a while. Greg was surprised. I told him that if I went ahead with my retirement the next year, my life would be boring. Then I added that I'd rather be bored in the office than bored somewhere else.

Greg didn't say any word.

Boring phone call indeed.

FRIENDS IN AND OUT

The front of our office had only a glass door and a large glass window. I made sure the back bay door was locked every day. There were no windows in our workspace.

The door separating my work area was kept open for me to see who was coming to the front door, and the door's chime was loud enough to alert me to straighten up from my nap.

During down time and to keep myself busy, I tended to my indoor plants. I had over ten kinds of plants enjoying my TLC. Being alone in a large workplace wasn't healthy, so to keep my sanity intact, I had to do something. Indoor plant gardening saved my sanity for many years. Every morning I had to chat with these creatures of beauty. I was always happy. Never did I hear any talking back to me. They were all content. A once-a-week watering was enough, and their habitation was strategically located just at the foot of the big glass windows facing the west. Perfect location.

One day I noticed with great interest that outside the front door, more friends were going by, such as rabbits, squirrels, birds, and dogs with their handlers. The types of bird that came and went included magpies, ravens, house birds, and others, whose names I don't know.

It gave me pleasure to see these birds flying in front of our office. The randomness and predictability of their everyday chores was a delight to observe. Then one afternoon an idea occurred to me. Birds and grain were best of friends, and we had a wealth of food supply in our storage area for these avian friends, along with lots of leftover bread.

Making friends with the birds wasn't hard. A handful of grain thrown outside the door from time to time attracted them with gusto. In no time, even their neighbours and families were invited to feast with the rest. They were my eye's delight, bringing with them different colours, sizes, and sounds.

I got my indoor plants to watch over them. Their joyful sound after being fed well suppressed my boredom.

My indoor and outdoor friends sustained my sanity and creativity.

OPEN AND DRAIN

This was the new lingo I learned from my dentist. One Thursday afternoon I was at my dentist's office. The scheduled visit was to remedy my aching front tooth.

I was used to the preliminaries of dental appointments. After many steps—one-minute mouth wash, spit over here, wear these sunglasses, make sure the cloth bib fits, so where's the tooth that troubling you, and do you still have insurance coverage—my dentist described the best healing scenario. The nerve in the tooth would have to be removed or neutralized. It was like a root canal but not with the intention of making it a more permanent fixture. She termed it "open and drain."

I asked if the procedure was painful, and she said yes. I prepared myself for this agonizing moment. Indeed, I felt the needle and jerked little. "I'm ok," I said. A few minutes passed, and she asked again of I could still feel pain. I asked her to put in more anesthetic. She complied. Another jab. Less jerking this time.

The drilling began. More drilling ensued. After thirty minutes or more, she gave me the antibiotic prescription. She added that three teeth needed extraction to start my long road to "dentureship"

In my head I entertained the idea that this procedure would be a significant opening and draining of pockets.

CHRISTMAS CONCERT
The first Christmas concert we attended was awesome, except!

My daughter invited us to watch it during the first week of December. She was picked up by her friends, and my wife and a friend would follow them. Outside it was dark, and a little snow was falling. The temperature was tolerable.

We left the house at 6:30 p.m. for the 7:00 p.m. event. I estimated a fifteen-minute drive would be enough to get a parking spot close to the main doors of the First Alliance Church in Calgary. Unfortunately, it took me three rounds around the parking lot. All spots were taken. I dropped off my wife and a friend at the front door and drove out of the compound. Along the street in front of the church, I saw a space for small car. Gotcha!

The area was still covered with snow. Snowfall in this part of the city was heavy. When I turned and headed to the spot, I saw an old man waving his arms metres in front of me. For him it was a close call. For me it was more of his mistake. My winter tires stopped well. I opened my window and shouted, "I'm sorry!"

With rage in his eyes, he responded by cursing. Then we both moved on.

The concert lasted an hour and a half. It was beautiful. Peoples' faces reflected joy and peace.

When the traffic wasn't heavy, I picked up my wife, friends, and now our daughter at the main door of the church. On our way back to the street, I shared my experience with them. All my passengers looked around with their eyes wide open for the guy I'd described to them.

METHANE READING

Our office was metres away from the park. The park, years back, was a dump area. Biomass and other biodegradable materials were buried there. Every year, per environmental bylaws, surrounding offices had to be tested for methane gas.

One quiet afternoon, the doorbell dinged. A young lady in a safety vest entered our door. With the instruments at hand, I knew what her task was. She started at the front office, then moved to the reception area. When she reached the lab room, where I was busy working on something, I asked her a question. She said, "Don't worry, this instrument won't register your gas."

We both lol.

CAPACITY

When the issuance of pandemic mandates was at its peak, our office walkways, walls, and doors were plastered with signs of all sizes, colours, messages, warnings, illustrations, and the like. The two-metre-distance warning wore out over time. What remained was the sign "Capacity limited to one person." There were five small rooms in our workplace. Five identical signs were still posted.

When my workmate retired, I was left alone. The stand-alone sanitizing machine begged for my hands to go under it every day. In one corner of the room, the cardboard box that could contain over ten thousand used masks always stared at me. The sanitizing wipes' plastic containers were permanent fixtures of every table. Others hadn't been opened yet. The opened ones were drying very fast.

Then one early morning in December, I debated with myself. Do I need to remove all this stuff to bring the workplace into a normal mode? Or must I wait for the final directive from head office?

The office was reduced to only one personnel, and there was no plan yet to bring in another person to work with me. Every time I entered one of the doors, I made sure no one was around to join me. Then I remembered I was the only one in the office. No masking or distancing needed.

HAIRDRESSER

Since the start of the pandemic, Trang had been our hairdresser. Her shop was metres away from the exit door of Walmart in Marlborough Mall in Calgary. My wife was impressed with how she cut my hair. I looked good after a thirty-day cycle because of her skill.

One cold afternoon a week before Christmas, I had to visit her. We were having our party that afternoon, and I only had a few hours to do all the chores my wife had listed for me to accomplish.

One person was in the queue. To kill the time, I went to the men's belt display. I could easily notice when the guy was done. I tried a number of belt styles and sizes, but most weren't genuine leather. Finally, after rummaging through the rest, I found one. I went to the till and paid without the hassle of waiting.

Moments later, Trang waved to me.

After our usual questions and answers, she started to share her experience from the week before. She'd been backing out of the parking lot when another car cut behind her. The incident looked like a typical accident. She and the other driver blamed the blind spot. But the story didn't stop there. A small crack in the back bumper of the other car was slightly visible. However, the guy demanded a cash compensation and no police involvement. They both knew that their insurance premiums would increase. The amount demanded was exorbitant, though. She said three thousand wasn't reasonable. They bargained and bargained more. Trang didn't want to spend her time settling the issue, and finally the guy settled for $800.00.

That was a case of blatant extortion, I thought to myself. I asked her where and what time she parked her car every day. Then I said, "I'll try to have you bump my car. Don't worry, I won't ask for over $100. I'll just demand three free haircuts."

"That sounds good to me," she said.

When I was backing out of the spot in the parking lot, I was reminded of Trang's experience. It made me even more cautious. The modus operandi of these people (the guy who demanded Trang's money) was well known in the community. Many called this group "cardemic" extortionists. They looked for opportunities to have their car damaged so they can demand large amounts of money and then pay a very small fraction of that at their own or co-conspirators' repair shop. A syndicate sort of.

This social ill would not deserve attention from the makers of the vaccine, I thought.

VIRAL
What have COVID, the flu, monkeypox, and RSV all done to the world? They all went viral!

HEROES' DAY
The idea of recognizing and appreciating all COVID-19 pandemic heroes (first responders, frontline health care professionals, and essential workers) in Alberta originated from my second book, *COVID-19 Fundemic*. On December 21, 2020, the first COVID-19 Pandemic Heroes' Day was declared by our group, Diaryo Alberta Society. Since then, over 2,750 pandemic heroes in the province have received certificates of recognition/appreciation and gift bags.

The inspiration for my second book and this one was borne out of my great respect and appreciation for the work and sacrifices of our pandemic heroes. More than ever, they were the ones who needed encouragement and inspiration to do just what they were doing. To add wit and humour to the equation would be a great service to them. Everyone knows that laughter is the best medicine—a medicine that produces healthier consequences than a vaccine of which the future effects are unknown.

BRAGGING RIGHTS

As the only one left in our workplace, I can boast now with full confidence that I am the best grain inspector in all Alberta—of course, my wife and daughter aren't convinced yet.

FOLLOWER

A good friend of mine for over twenty years was a registered psychologist. His retirement years were a turning point in his career. From many years of service with the city's Family Services, his new gig as volunteer counsellor in one of the support institutions in the city was quite satisfying. Arleigh was a devout Christian and heavily involved in his church. A guest lecturer, preacher, and seminar presenter, he was never bored. His doctrinal, theological, and psychological understanding of the Bible was phenomenal. He was my de facto counsellor and mentor.

The best ways of getting in touch with him were his cell phone and email. At home, three TV channels suited his lifestyle perfectly well. When we visited his place years back, it was cluttered with books, literature, journals, and other mind-boggling materials. I never dared ask about his singlehood.

His passion was classical music. With other friends, we enjoyed our time together watching opera and classical plays at the Jack Singer Concert Hall and Jubilee Auditorium.

His career experience, educational preparations, and church engagement solidified his conservative values. Going to movies, social events, and other social gatherings weren't his cup of tea. He'd rather stay home and watch his TV programs on his forty-five-inch TV located in one corner of his living room floor with cluttered books around it.

On Christmas Eve of 2022, our friend and neighbour invited us for a dinner. Hours before the scheduled celebration, she suggested that I invite our friend Arleigh. At that time, Arleigh was waiting for a call from one of his friends to go over to their place for a dinner. In our phone call, he told me to email him the address of our friend, Lisa. *Better that way*, I said to myself. Hours later, he confirmed his coming.

Our dinner was set at 7:30. It was 7:50 when he appeared on the front doorstep. Like me, driving at night in a new area of the city can be disorientating for him, and he missed Lisa's place.

Our dinner was great. The baked salmon was enticing, the chicken and ham delightful, the buttered corn refreshing, and the wonton soup perfect. Halfway through our dinner, Arleigh confessed his dislike for the smell and taste of fried pork and cheese. He narrated his experiences with these foods with feeling and great effect. Okay, we got it.

Before dessert, our conversation tuned to his past career and present retirement chores. His doctoral dissertation had something to do with the drug user's anger management and family violence. Lately, he'd been one of the counsellors dealing with the issues of battered woman. Psychological intervention was needed, as he always advocated.

Our conversation shifted to famous people in politics, religion, and entertainment who were directly related to the topics of his expertise. Our friend Lisa was curious to dig into other info from Arleigh. Her experiences on the issue weren't a secret to us. She treated us as her family. His explanation enlightened not only Lisa but my wife and I as well.

The worst thing about substance abuse, family violence, and an abusive partner is the result: harm to the person, depression, and death through suicide or by the partner (violent confrontation). These consequences were documented, studied, and used to develop interventions.

The direction of the conversation headed to suicide. The stories of Robin Williams, Cade, Bourdin, and many other prominent people and celebrities were unfamiliar to Arleigh. He didn't know these people, as the entertainment world was not part of his daily intake of information. But his dislike for Trump was intense. A crooked and mean man, as he always uttered.

Then my wife mentioned another person who'd committed suicide. With his eyes wide and voice elevated, Arleigh asked, "tWitch? The Black guy who was good at dancing?" Lisa, my wife, and I hid our surprise at his surprise. My wife and Lisa patiently shared the news with him with added feeling. That was the recap of our dinner talk.

He said thank you and headed back to his parked car half a block away.

As we helped Lisa put away things from the table, we all had a good laugh. We thought he knew very little about White movie and television personalities. When the name of tWitch (Stephen Boss) was mentioned, he quickly recognized the guy. We guessed only Arleigh knew the answer to why "tWitch" was known to him.

During that time with Arleigh, we never touched on or discussed the pandemic at all. It was liberating!

BOSS

A week before the end of 2022, I inquired about the plan for our office. It was mid-November when my workmate retired. Since then, I'd been by myself in the office. My scheduled holiday was the first week of January until mid-February. Somebody had to be in the office to take care of the daily tasks: receiving work from the mail, unannounced producers dropping off samples, and building operators. The office had to be open during my holiday.

In the middle of the week, my supervisor from Saskatchewan called. We discussed the updated plan for the office. Not much of a surprise, but it was confirmed that my previous supervisor, who'd retired five years ago, would come and "babysit the office." Details of his on-call duty were elaborated for me. He was given ninety days to cover the days I'd be out or on holiday for the first quarter of the year.

The expectations included training and refreshing him on the new systems in our office. Most likely the challenge would fall on the area of computer use, online stuff, and other systems updates.

The next day, Bill, my former supervisor, called. We talked, exchanged pleasantries, and went straight to his roles. He confirmed the one plan I'd heard from our regional manager from Vancouver.

Bill had been gone from the office for over four years, yet I still called him Boss. This boss thing was for my own interpretation and use. I haven't divulged to anyone the real reason why I call him boss.

At first, I was filled with angst over the arrangement. In the back of my head, I said, "I'd rather work alone than have Bill around." Though his on-call position level was the same as mine, I still had a feeling of being under his watch.

Well, I just hoped that when I got back from my holiday, a box of chocolates would make a difference in the only office of our company in Alberta.

For a ninety-day period.

NEW YEAR'S EVE STORIES

Our friend invited us to celebrate New Year's Eve with her at her cousin's place in the deep southwest quadrant of Calgary. I estimated the drive would just be under thirty minutes. The seven o'clock gathering was planned hastily, with last-minute invitations given to relatives scattered around the city.

While enjoying our time on the road, we inquired if it was okay that we were going with our friend. My wife insisted that she knew the lady who owned the house. A big house, indeed. Our friend assured us that everything would be ok.

The front porch and walkway weren't shoveled, and a half foot of snow covered the steps leading to the main door. The driveway on the west side of the house was clear of snow. Safety first. The door opened after two rings. Sniffing out the opened door was this big, brown-spotted male dog. We could hear the banging of his tail against the wall. The aroma of Filipino dishes stuck to our nostril in no time. The shoe rack at the back of the closet was cramped with different colours, sizes, and smell of footwear.

Two guys were seriously watching an action movie in the first living room. On the floor- elevated kitchen, women were prepping the food. The long table in the next room was filled with different dishes. Beef steak cut into strips and cubes perked up my appetite. Other Filipino dishes were scattered on the table too.

Moments later, Amy, a woman in her mid-sixties motioned and invited us to grab a seat at the dinning table. Once we were all seated, the five-year gracious and generous widow started to share her life story. By the looks and reception of the people around us, I had this inclination that everyone in the room knew her story by heart.

Married to a Caucasian many years back, her colourful life journey inspired many of her family members and relatives. From her start as a caregiver to a career that had brought her to the present moment, it was a story worth hearing.

Her unassuming, simple, and humble husband was the solid financial rock, known only after his death. Four rental houses and other valuable items at home kept Amy and their only son, Felix, secure. No wonder her house size, location, and the items in the house were above ordinary. What was more compelling was her life story way back in the Philippines. From rags to riches.

We both enjoyed her life story, the food, and how she coped with the onslaught of the pandemic that nearly cost her life.

PHILIPPINE HOLIDAY

The months spent planning our vacation to our homeland, the Philippines, were full of moments to remember. The first week of January was a busy time for us. In my workplace, I found out that my vacation time left only equalled 1.74 hours. My five-week holiday credit would start in April 2023.

All our bags were packed and ready to go. The luggage my daughter bought was big enough for all the items she wanted us to bring back home for her. She handed us pictures of the items she wanted. We assured her that we wouldn't go wrong with the list.

I listed four goals in making the trip. First was to attend our high school reunion to mark its forty-eighth year. Second was my kids' plan to invest in real estate in our hometown. Both had the resources, but we didn't know where to start. The target was the old vacation house of some of my wife's older relatives. The place was ideal in terms of size, height, and proximity to the national highway. Meeting olds friends would be one of the most anticipated moments.

CALGARY TO VANCOUVER

Our daughter drove and dropped us off at the YYC airport three hours before our flight in the early morning of January 8. We approached one of the weighing stations to make sure our luggage met the weight requirement. They were all bang on. The family standing close to us had difficulty deciding what items weren't needed. Minutes into the chaos, they finally settled on just leaving one of the boxes. We said hi to them, and off we went on the long walk leading to the departure area. I thought the walk was only a short distance, but my daughter told me differently.

Fifteen minutes later, with our new friend, we settled into one of the rows of comfy chairs. We talked and shared a bit about ourselves, including where we lived, our job status, and whether we were retired or not.

The woman felt comfortable with my wife. With no hesitation, she shared that her marriage to a Sudanese guy was not that rosy. I lost interest listening to her story of intrigue, shame, and suspicions. The topic changed, and my wife pointed at the hard liquor bag at the lady's feet, asking why she'd bought hard liquor at the duty-free shop.

The woman's family saga was not only confined to Calgary. The same nature of discontent and conflict were also present in the Philippines. The wine she'd bought was for her alcoholic and wealthy brother-in-law. *This woman must be an enabler*, I thought. With a smile on her face, she said, "to hasten his demise or death. Family problem solved." We all lol.

We boarded right on time. The just over one-hour flight to Vancouver was normal at best.

The over-an-hour flight between Calgary and Vancouver was a warmup drill. The snack of pretzels, cookies, and a drink wasn't bad. It added energy and calories to our bodies. WestJet was known for this short flight offering. As expected, we arrived on time.

VANCOUVER TO HONG KONG

In Vancouver, our trek from the WestJet domestic terminal to Cathay Pacific International terminal was no joke. Our Calgary walk paled in comparison to this one. We established familiarity with the other passengers, most of whom were headed to the same gate and plane as us. One frustrating issue was that our layover time was only two hours. By the look of it, we had to double time our stride. The family we were following was hard to catch up to.

More turns, excuses, and "let this guy pass first" moments. We just kept on following them like puppies. Just as our gasping for air intensified, we finally arrived at the end gate of the terminal. The demography changed considerably. Chinese nationals dominated the crowd.

One of the plane attendants behind the booth approached us with a smile. She led us to the computer station and requested our vaccination record, boarding pass, and passport. Minutes later, we were told to get back to where she'd picked us up.

The long wait finally ended, and the flight attendant standing at the plane's door directed us to our seat. Carry-on luggage on the overhead compartment, buckled up, we looked around and sighed.

Tracy was a retiree/senior from British Columbia who took her seat next to me. Her destination was Thailand for a five-week holiday. We exchanged smiles.

The plane took off. The cabin quieted. The seat belt signs were on. The over twelve-hour flight was the only thing I remembered from the captain's announcement.

Another smile to Tracy and the conversation started. I told her that we'd been planning our trip for a long time. I learned that her trip was to attend the funeral of Thailand's queen. News like this seldom made international coverage, especially from Thailand. More probing questions and more insightful sharing. She told me her secret. Work hard while you can, save as much as you can, and quit. For over twenty years, she'd been retired and enjoying the fruit of being a real estate agent.

I intently absorbed her wisdom, nodded, and then in no time dozed off. A little bump interrupted my snoring. However, Tracy napped like a baby. Her snoring was at lower decibel.

The Cathay's food was way different from my daily meals. Quite a treat, my wife and Tracy affirmed.

The twelve-hour flight was arduous, stressful, and no fun. Netflix was a good companion. Three movies, news, and other programming lulled my mind, and I forgot I was over 30,000 feet over the edge of the Pacific Ocean.

The landing was uneventful, again. Familiar faces came to view. The families in front and behind us had travelled with us this far.

A five-hour layover at Hong Kong International Airport was great. More stretching, walking around, and cat napping proved relaxing. My nap ended when I remembered I had to respond to emails, so I took my laptop and headed straight to one of the computer tables closest to the glass window. The opposite table with a computer terminal was occupied by a young lady, who smiled at me. We found out she was a Filipina who'd been in Manila for two weeks with her family. She was now heading home to Halifax. Her story resonated with a sad note. Her holiday to the Philippines proved refreshing and insightful, but she wasn't close and buddy-buddy with her dad. The gap between them was big, and her only source of support was her uncle and aunt in the Philippines.

My wife, with her mother's instinct, gave her nuggets of wisdom and relational tools. They talked longer while I went to the washroom.

We invited her to dine with us, but she declined. Understood. However, she gave us a bottle of carbonated water. I gave her my coordinates and promised to connect to her.

There were only few food stores opened. The one with the long line was worth the wait. I ordered two of their specials. As we enjoyed our last bite, we saw people from the store carrying a different kind of food not found on the menu. The food was wrapped in a leaf. We were familiar with that food, but we didn't know the Chinese name for it. If we'd known how to read Chinese characters, we would have ordered the same. Too late the hero.

The clock said we had one more hour before departing. We followed the directions to our departure gate, which wasn't in the building. It was in the other building to our left, connected by a passageway. We asked the other passengers in front of us, in our dialect, of course, and our departure time and gate number were the same.

The same procedures, the same routine, and we settled into our respective seat assignment in the plane. One thing we'd learned so far: Don't hesitate to ask, go with the flow, and smile.

HONG KONG TO MANILA

The time to relax and the snack were short-lived. We always made sure our carry-on bags, which were heavy, were within our sight and reach. We took turns connecting and interacting with people. First, we told people that we were new retirees. When assistance was needed, I had to intentionally imbalance my walk a little bit. The airline staff were cognizant of this and accommodating. The young family before us was our guide. Following them metres away proved effective. We had no time to ask other people where to go, and we observed that this family had been frequent travellers to Manila.

The running of time and the speed of our walk yielded a very tiring and stressful trek. Though we memorized the steps and items for the next leg of our trip, we weren't that close to doing it right.

At the end of the long hallway was a long line of people. The gate number was bright and clear. We sighed with relief. We reached our designated gate, where the crowd was big. One of the customer agents approached behind the line and ushered us to the boarding table. We produced our vaccine records and identifying documents. In no time we were told to get back to the line. Moments later, boarding commenced. Seniors' privileges kicked in. Again we were ushered into the front of the line with other seniors.

My last international flight had been twelve years ago. The plane looked new. Over three hundred people patiently located their respective seat assignment. Once I placed our carry-on bags in the compartment, I saw the family ten rows back from us. We waved and smiled.

The captain's announcement quieted the cabin, and the plane moved quietly and positioned itself for take off. The thrust and force of the Cathay Pacific engine was so strong. The plane ascended quickly and stabilized after a few minutes in the air.

After roughly thirty minutes in the air, we had a good time savouring the meals that had been served. Just over halfway through the trip, my mood changed. No Netflix. The local TV programs and channels weren't that exciting. Old movie selections were not appealing. Retirees or seniors like us wouldn't waste time watching older (than us) flicks.

From a distance, I saw the smoky skyline of Metro Manila. The cabin temperature changed dramatically.

The arrival at the Ninoy Aquino International Airport was not eventful. Now the demographics changed. As we reached the end of the tube, I saw two Cathay Pacific agents. Printed in bold font was my name and the name of one other person. With a smile on my face, I asked the guy holding the paper, "I'm not a Hollywood personality, so what's up?" Our luggage had been left behind in Calgary. To our dismay, I had to talk to the person in charge of the baggage claim department. They were just the people at the receiving end. There were no other explanations given.

As we moved with the crowd, it occurred to me what kind of gift I had to give to our relatives. The brightly-lit duty-free shop was just metres away from the last gate leading to the waiting area. One of the offerings for that day was a package. Four Johnny Walkers and a small piece of carry-on luggage attracted my attention. That was the first time I shelled out over a hundred American dollars. The very first time I used my credit card in a foreign land.

The WIFI in the airport allowed me to messenger chat with my in-laws. They'd been in the area for quite some time, waiting for us. I tried to locate gate number six once outside the building, and indeed, one of the big pillars outside had a number six printed on it. Off we went to stand close to it. Another chat and still no visible contact. Another instruction. This time I was told their car was parked just at the north end of the terminal, close to Robins Donuts. At the end of the terminal there was no Robins. We chatted again for the fourth time. This time Greg, the husband of my in-law, Nora, was standing close to the security staff at one of the main entrance doors.

Our waiting was over. They weren't waiting for us out there in the open street. They'd parked the van at the indoor parking lot of the airport at sector six. That experience cost us around sixty minutes of our holiday.

The drive from Terminal 3 to San Pedro, Laguna took only forty-five minutes. Before the bypass was built, it would have taken us over two hours, said Greg. I glanced at the speed our driver was going and was impressed. Over one hundred kilometres per hour. The Manila I knew over thirty years ago was far different. My observation that first night was that the volume of traffic and pollution had more than doubled below the bypass highway. The highway leading out of the metropolis was littered with buildings, with no empty spaces in between. As we entered San Pedro City, we noted that the streets were narrow. No two cars could pass each other without slowing down. For the hundreds, or even thousands, of tricycles, and the mass public transit, the narrow streets were their playground. Carlos, our driver, turned right into one of the subdivisions in the city. The seventh house from the gate to left was our destination.

We had a good talk and a late dinner.

We woke up late the next morning, but the table was ready. I grabbed one small banana from the fruit tray. Years earlier I'd eaten this variety, and my senses and palate remembered those early years. We talked at the table about our itinerary for the next day.

MALL OF ASIA (MOA)

Early the following morning, Pastor Michael wondered at my hair. Booking a home service wasn't a problem in Manila, even in less than twenty-four hours. I looked better, said my wife. We shelled out over 50 per cent of his rate, plus I gave him a pen from work.

After hours of rituals, we were all ready to head out.

The Mall of Asia (MOA) was once the biggest in Asia. We reached it close to noon time. Our breakfast was good but not enough to sustain us for more hours. Kenny Roger's chicken caught my in-laws' attention. The small and narrow restaurant was filled with people. As we were placing our order, a table at the back was vacated. I paid, took the order number, and we occupied the table.

More talking.

It was mid-afternoon when we entered SM's Kultura store. All the items on display were reflections, representations, and in recognition of Filipino culture. From men's and women's attire, accessories, wrapped candies and assortments of food, and house displays—all were culturally related. My wife proceeded straight to the women's clothing display. Over one hour of grabbing samples from the rack, trying them on, bargaining, and trading was time well spent for her. I nursed my sore legs while standing, walking, and waiting within the vicinity. My wife sensed my agony, so she led me to the men's shoe area. I couldn't say no to the brand of shoe we'd agreed to buy before, even in Canada. Got it, paid, and sighed.

The total bill was over $200 Canadian plus a 5 per cent surcharge fee. I could still smell the chicken laced in my credit card. *We should have brought peso currency*, I thought. Our excuse and rationale were that we were contributing to the economy of the country. Fair, we thought.

Very few, I observed, wore masks and practised distancing in and outside the mall.

SAN PEDRO TO MUNOZ

The next day we were all set and ready for a long trip and a scheduled lunch with a good friend in Pulilan, Bulacan. Along the way, we stopped at one of the branches of Cebuana Money Remittance Office. My daughter advised us of the money she'd sent the night before. Cool. The stack of Filipino pesos was thick. My wife had little difficulty securing it in her purse.

The drive from San Pedro to Pulilan took just under one hour. Our first exit was wrong, but the next one was the right exit. We followed Lou's, our friend's, directions. If not for the narrowness and challenging street curves, we would have arrived earlier.

Lou's house was cute and clean. There was no grass around it because the front and side were both paved. Tony, Lou's hubby, welcomed us with a serious expression, as though asking, "Who are these people?" After greetings and introductions, we were led to another fenced, house-size shed, a receiving facility for family and friends gathering. The smell of BBQ and other food on the table intensified our hunger. Everyone loved the boiled peanut. At twenty-nine degrees outside, the cold drink was welcomed with gusto.

Tony's rock-solid demeanour was hard to crack. After a few trial balloons, the stiffness in his face loosened considerably. The next thing I knew, we were all lol.

Before we departed from their place, we agreed on a plan. The couple would join us to visit Manilungao National Park and Pantabangan Dam.

THE REUNION

The time to assemble was set at ten in the morning. My excitement compelled me to wake up early and be ready one hour before heading to the venue.

I was dropped off half a block away, as there was no parking spot in front of the house. Inside the fence were three ten-by-ten-foot tents, courtesy of the city mayor.

The woman behind the registration table looked familiar. Our eyes met, we smiled, and at the same time asked each other's name. We both laughed out loud. More of these scenes ensued. Reminiscing about the past brought joy and nostalgia. Vivid memories of the past were endearing to everyone.

Even our invited former teachers were so happy to meet us. Anthea, over ninety years old, had been my English teacher. I told her in front of many others around the table how she shaped my love for reading and writing. Before their very eyes I signed and handed my book, *Open Visa*, to Anthea. She couldn't believe that one of her students' passions was writing.

The reunion struck me with two obvious realities. One, the younger face resemblance of the people around was still vivid. Two, just like anyone there, I had difficulty remembering names.

AUNT LIGAYA

Five houses down the street, north of where we stayed, lived a well-respected elderly woman. She was the first cousin of my wife's mother. It was customary for many people to visit her and just say hi. Her generosity knew no bounds. One's visit would mean a valuable gift afterwards, such as a sack of rice, vegetables, canned foods, etc.

After I was re-introduced, our conversation was interrupted by the loud siren of an ambulance. We ignored it. Again, another ambulance sounded, heading in the opposite direction. Nana Ligaya said that if the ambulance was headed to San Jose City, that would be good news. If the direction was Cabanatuan City, where the Provincial General Hospital was located, it was no doubt COVID. We looked at each other and digested her observation.

As we headed off from the house with two sacks of rice, another ambulance approached, going in the direction of San Jose. We sighed with relief.

MINALUNGAO NATIONAL PARK

Located in the southeast side of the province, in the town of Gen. Tino, the park was one of the most sought-after hide-aways for people desiring to get closer to nature. It took us roughly three and a half hours to get there. The volume of traffic, the number of obstructions along the way, and the structural challenges posed by the highways slowed travel time and tried the patience of many of us. Just a kilometre away from the site, our vehicle was stopped by people on the roadside. The gate going into the park was closed indefinitely. There was no point arguing with them. We were just visitors in the area and tens of kilometres away from the police station in town. Their advice was easy to follow.

We took a right turn to one of the resorts adjacent to the river. Down the hill we parked and settled in one of the sheds. More downstream steps took us to where the bamboo rafts were parked. From a distance, was saw the end portion of the park. The park was desolate, indeed. There were people walking around, but we guessed they were the locals. The question remained in our minds: Would we be able to just touch the rocks separating the park from the rest of the resorts?

The operator of the resort indicated we could. The bamboo rafts down would enable us to cross the river. From there we could walk to the park in five to ten minutes. That was good.

I looked at the time. Lou and Tony were nowhere near the area. The signal was poor and choppy. The resort operator advised me to walk farther up the hill, which I did, and Lou's text appeared. They were roughly forty-five minutes away from us.

Our wait ended after an hour. The couple got out of the car, exhausted and looking hungry. The table was ready ahead of their arrival, so they grabbed their food and joined us.

After our meal we prepped ourselves for the raft ride and walk to the park. Though the noon temp was roving in the thirties, we had a good time riding and walking. Moments later we reached the edge of the park, where big boulders invited us for a selfie. We were able to reach and sneak into and between the rocks for our selfie.

Waiting for us down the path back to where we came from was the guy in charge of the area. He wasn't a park warden or security. He told us to clear the area and go back to our resort. No big deal; we complied.

Upon reaching our shed in the resort, we discussed how to communicate this issue to the National Park office. The park was national, owned by the national government. There was no way it could be closed to the public except for some very important reason. Our discussion was cut short by the resort operator when he heard our conversation and when we asked him why the park was closed. He explained that the road leading to the park in this end was owned by the mayor, who had lost his seat in the last election.

We stared at each other. That was why. We left the resort later in the afternoon.

PANTABANGAN DAM

Known to be the biggest dam in the mid-70s, Pantabangan Dam was over two and a half hours away from the science city of Munoz. Our mid-morning travel was perfectly timed for our lunch arrival.

The first thing on our list was the dam itself. Minutes into the town proper, we turned left. The winding road led us to the main gate leading to the dam. The traffic pole was down, and a guy came out of the office wearing a white shirt with the National Irrigation Administration logo etched on the left corner. Joie, not only the most vocal but also the most assertive woman in the group, tried her best to convince the guy behind the pole to let us pass. Her persuasion skill was no match for the staff. In defeat, we all turned around and drove back to the main highway.

Our next stop was Lake Farm De la Marre Resort. The parking lot was half-full when we reached the place. The entrance fee wasn't bad, and the shed assigned to us was great in that it overlooked the valley and the lake north of the resort.

Moments later, to my surprise, a group of people headed our way. I recognized the faces. They were five of my classmates from 1975 in high school, all wearing big smiles. We were neighbours, and we exchanged greetings. All seniors now, we talked about life, our past memorable moments in high school, our crushes, and even the few teachers who'd terrorized us. We spent the time in the resort sharing many fond memories and stories. Tony and Lou enjoyed our company, the place, the scenery, the travel, and the food.

The impact of the pandemic was downplayed. It was hard for others to share about their respective bouts with COVID. The emotional and financial toll was high and devastating. One thing we all agreed upon and upheld was that the time left for us should be spent on things and moments like this one—spending time with friends and enjoying God's creation in front of us.

At the end of the day, we found out that the closing of the dam leading to the village of Fatima was political in nature. As we drove back home, it occurred to me how serious politics were in my homeland. Many more issues bubbled up, including the unsettled debate about the pandemic protocols and health-related mandates. All boiled down to politics.

THE INVITE

The front lawn of the executive house was well lit. The food table over-flowed. People occupying the tables were busy exchanging pleasantries. After grace was said, we all stood and lined up at the food table.

I greatly appreciated many of my old friends' and colleagues' greet-ings. Many of them were newly retired, and others still held high pos-itions within the university. As we were feasting, the celebrant, the presi-dent of Central Luzon State University (CLSU), walked to our table. I was glad Dr. Edgar Orden remembered my name. I quickly shared with him my memory of his late dad—my professor way back then. My hands-on training on caponizing a chicken was successful. I took off the stuff from the side of the chicken perfectly. However, minutes later, the chicken died. We all lol.

I felt nostalgic and wondered what my status would have been had we not immigrated to Canada over thirty years ago. The invite gave me another insight on life. Irrespective of status, the spirit of friendship remained open, timeless, and even enduring.

One thing was observable, though. Nobody cared about the distance or masks that night.

SSS (SOCIAL SECURITY SYSTEM) CONTRIBUTION

"That will be 1,750.00 Pesos, Po," said the lady behind window four at the Social Security Service office in San Jose City. This was the amount of my previous employer's contribution to my SSS benefit.

My wife and I stared at each other with a mixed reaction. "What?" she said.

"What the …?" I said.

The lady added, "When you pass away, sir, your wife is entitled to no more than 15,000.00 Pesos." If I started contributing more, I'd have more insurance coverage for my wife. We looked at each other again.

We headed out of the SSS office and entered the grocery store to our left. We explored the store and in no time mentally calculated some figures. The amount that my wife would receive if I passed was only good for ten shopping sprees.

We left the store with 500 pesos worth of merchandise, maskless and bit cautious.

PHILIPPINE CARABAO RESEARCH

The guard was polite but insisted that my friend, who'd driven us there, produce her ID. After a brief call, he allowed us to proceed. As our car moved, I looked back at the guard house. Indeed, the guy took note of our plate number. We followed the directions given us, and a young lady was waiting for us in the lobby.

The office of Dr. Claro Mingala, the director designate of Philippine Carabao Research, was elaborate, big, and with bookshelves all around. Our joy was complete when one of his staff came into the room with a snack. A second guy put a medium-size Styrofoam cooler down in front of us. The milk, choco-milk, yogurt, and other carabao-milk-based products levelled up our enjoyment and gratitude.

With pride, Dr. Mingala drove us to one of the field labs behind the building. For health and safety reasons, the compound was guarded. Every vehicle or person entering the gate had to be registered. The security guard followed the procedures to the letter. Even when my nephew took off his mask, he insisted to have Dr. Claro's ID handed to him. I wondered if the guard ever read the title of the guy on the ID. Just the same, he took note of the vehicle's plate number.

Joie, our friend who had driven us to the PCRC, opened the window and in a loud voice informed the guard, "Don't you know he's your director here in this centre?" The guard just scratched his head.

There were close to 350 heads of carabao under the two sheds. We learned so many things about the centre. The milking was done mechanically now, and the farrowing, feeding, and even culling were new to us.

Back in front of the small guard house, the guy stood straight, saluted, and said, "Sorry, sir, I'm just new in this job."

We all smiled, and Dr. Claro put on his mask again.

MT. SAMAT

The place was a memorial to fallen soldiers during WWII. On top of Mt. Samat was a tall, concrete, white cross. The parking lot was full when we reached the place. We got out of the car and went straight to the tourists' and visitors' briefing room.

The five-minute orientation was very informative and helpful. The tail end of our time in the briefing room was the question-and-answer time. I looked around and saw that over 50 per cent of the guests were seniors, retirees, or over fifty years old. I asked, "Does the facility have elevators or escalators?" Nope. I then asked if the park had a First Aid kiosk along the route going to the big cross, or anywhere on the over ten-hectare memorial park. Nope again. The answers changed our plan. We decided not to walk around the steep slope and pathways of the park. Instead, we spent our time at the foot of the museum and at the side of a big canon facing Manila Bay. We took a lot of selfies.

LAS CASAS

Known for its exotic legacy and Spanish-era houses, Las Casas Filipinas De Acuzar was just hours away from Mt. Samat. A beach resort, convention centre, and heritage destination rolled into one (lacasasfilipinas.com).

The information centre was just metres away from the main entrance. Visitors and tourists milled around the front, inside, and back of the information building. We opted to just walk around and enjoy the scenery. Others registered for the group tour. Included in our entrance fee was the lunch provided in one of the buildings close to the beach. One of the highlights of our visit was a boat ride. The canals threading the different legacy houses made the ride interesting and convenient.

As I looked around, I saw the legacy houses scattered around and separated only by the water-filled canals. Before we hopped on the boat, I asked the guide why they offered the boat ride without any life jackets on board. Then I followed with, "Are you a certified lifeguard?"

The guy just smiled and politely answered, "The water isn't deep, and the ride is safe."

We had the best time in Las Casas. The history, scenery, people, food, and esthetic nature of the resort was unparalleled.

It was late in the afternoon when we headed back home. Halfway to our destination, it occurred to me how lax the operators of tourist destinations like Mt. Samat Memorial and Las Casas were in terms of health and safety.

EXPRESSWAY

The year 2010 was my last visit to the Philippines, and at that time I noticed many physical and social changes in the country. The traffic remained heavy, and the population kept on climbing. However, the construction of a bigger, longer highway running north to south on the main island, Luzon, was impressive.

The major highways include Central Luzon Link Expressway (CLLEX), Manila–Cavite Expressway (CAVITEX), Muntinlupa–Cavite Expressway (MCX), NAIA Expressway (NAIAX), NLEX Harbor Link, North Luzon Expressway (NLEX), Metro Manila Skyway, and South Luzon Expressway (SLEX). Indeed, we've experienced driving on some of these major arteries. Impressive, fast, and convenient thoroughfares.

One night my wife asked my opinion on our highways in Alberta compared with the express highways in the Philippines. In Alberta we have very few major highways: Highway #1, Highway #2, and Yellowhead

Highway. In the Philippines they have many. However, there was one thing I really missed. "What's that?" my wife asked. During our holidays we had more time surfing on those highways than I did on Netflix!

THE VISIT

Weeks before our arrival from the Philippines, our former colleagues at the Central Luzon State University planned to visit one of our dear friends, so we secured one of the town coaches. I was the only guy, except the two drivers, of the sixteen passengers. They were all retirees, twelve had PhDs, and they all held various professorial positions in the university. Glad to know that positions don't matter anymore in the realm of retirement. Given all other matters, we all looked and talked the same.

The trek was long and tiring. To keep the group alive while in transit and after a long nap, Joie started a conversation. For over an hour the hottest topic was people's time with Netflix. I was not alone on that matter, indeed.

WHY NOT?

My wife's eldest sister's family was big. The second time we visited her family compound, we were swarmed with kids, teens, and even adults. Noticeably, there was a three-year-old Black boy there, who'd been adopted by one of my sister-in-law's daughters. We just listened, nodded, and asked no questions. The kid's story was sad and intriguing.

Back at our home base later that night, the subject of the adopted boy surfaced. Our friend, not privy to the situation, insinuated their dislike of the arrangement. We all knew that there were over ten children in the compound. Adding one more would be too much for the elders, and more for my sister-in-law to manage and feed. The care, attention, and feeding became the contentious reasons why my friends resented the idea of adoption.

The following morning, we heard our friend calling all her pets. One dog and nine cats. I asked her why she had so many cats, and she said that it would be cruel to relocate the cats out in the field or in a faraway place. It would be pitiful to neglect, abandon, and deny the chance to love these pets. When the cats were fed and mellowed their meowing, it occurred to me that there were similarities between the adopted kid and the cats. In the back of my mind, I'd rather give the boy the chance to live and be loved by a family than having so many cats littering and loitering around.

EL NIDO

One of the most popular places for tourists in the Philippines is El Nido. located on the north side of the Palawan Island. The agency that facilitated our hastily-planned trip was based in Luzon. The three-day and two-night trip cost lots of money and created unforgettable memories. The one-hour flight from Manila to El Nido airport went well. Indeed, waiting for us outside the gate of the small airfield was a guy with my name printed on a paper. Other people in group tour lined up and got into their respective twelve-seater vans. Others were fetched by SUVs, minivans, and air-conditioned vehicles.

My wife and I followed the guy. In the middle of the unpaved and dusty parking lot was a three-wheeled limousine, fondly called "Tricycle." He secured our stuff in the back carrier, and we barely fit inside the not-so-well-maintained, stained, ripped up, upholstered chair. Our bums settled and fit into the chair after many bumps and humps on the road. The seven-kilometre ride was a blast. The long, narrow, rolling, dusty, smoky, and crappy provincial highway made our stress worse.

The tricycle ride ended with no untoward incident. The receptionist at the El Nido Beach Resort couldn't find our names on the list of expected guests arriving that day, so I called our travel agent. Moments later, a guy appeared out of nowhere and talked to the lady behind the desk. With the issue clarified, we were directed to occupy one of the rooms on the second floor. We had to change attire fast, as we only had twenty minutes before our island-hopping scheduled that day.

Dante, the guy in charge of our day's activity, led us to another office along the narrow and crowded street. Many people who looked lost like us were waiting for more instructions. A lady in her mid fifties, if our assessment was right, walked us to the beach. She was small, slim, with short hair, and two teeth missing.

Smiles of vendors greeted us warmly. All sorts of island-hopping merchandise and items flashed before our faces. Our contact lady led us to another lady with boxes of goggles and water shoes in front of her. Our arguments against renting water shoes were defeated. Our running shoes were of no use on the sharp and edgy solid rocks underneath the waves of the ocean. The rental fee wasn't bad, we rationalized.

Minutes into waiting, we got the signal from the other guy. Our boat was anchored at the floating dock waiting for us. Five crew members and nine guests, all Filipinos, were the normal capacity for this trip.

The first island was twenty-five minutes away. The cove was fantastic. Our tour guide, a young guy with a knack for speaking English and a sense of humour, paddled us to a safe place in one corner of the cove. Hidden huge rock crevices were perfect for the call of nature. An hour in the water paddling around was a new experience for us, but it cost us 300 pesos. After three islands, the scenery became stale and looked similar. There were no washrooms on the islands either. We were the last to get off the boat and do what we needed to do while we were at the steps with half our body under the salt water.

On to the next island for our lunch. We had to walk from the boat into the neck-deep water. The water shoes were very useful, as they protected our feet from the sharp, rugged, and uneven underwater rock terrain. The crew brought in the table and the food. Once set up, one of the senior men requested the group to say grace for the food. No one volunteered, so I prompted him to do it. We all said amen after his short prayer.

Everyone enjoyed the shrimp, oyster, crab, tuna, chicken barbeque, and fruits (mango, grapes, banana, and watermelon). We brought our own bottled water. Two more stop-over islands to explore brought different scenery, but they were all just surrounded by water. We were all weary and ready to go back to the shore.

We were sweaty, salty, sticky, and stressed out when we reached the shore. Back at our hotel we took a shower and clinched a short nap, then we got ready for a much-awaited dinner. The narrow street was crammed with people, mostly tourists and vendors. Our walk led us to a pizza joint.

The next day's island hopping mirrored the first day. Late in the afternoon, the narrow street was crammed with people, mostly tourists and vendors. Our walk led us to a different restaurant. We enjoyed the local adobo version and fresh coconut water.

A new and costly experience, indeed.

IMPRESSIVE

AirSwift was the only commercial plane with a private airport in El Nido. It was a turbo prop but equally right on time for the departure and arrival.

It was late in the evening when our flight arrived at the domestic airport in Manila from El Nido. The domestic terminal was clean, tidy, and well kept. Once inside, we were impressed by the system of the luggage carousel. Around it were luggage carts evenly spaced. Passengers didn't need to grab one from a corner of the building. Impressive.

I approached the two young attendants in the arrival area. They appreciated my commendation for their work in making sure the carts were in place and ready for use by us. The guy pushed the red button but there was no carousel movement. After the third time, there was still no movement. We were advised to move to the next carousel. Finally, luggage started to emerge from the chute. I looked at the two attendants, smiled, and said, "Good job, folks, except the machine."

Off we went out of the terminal to wait for our ride. I looked back inside and saw the two young attendants quickly setting up the carts around the two carousels.

BAGS ARE PACKED

Our flight back home took off at eight in the morning on February 8, 2023. This time we had to check in four big pieces of luggage.

We left my sister-in-law's place around 3:30 a.m. and arrived in front of the NAIA terminal 4 and blended in with the big crowd of passengers flying out of Manila. We were the first in line at the check-in counter. To our surprise, I had to pay $450.00 US for the extra luggage. I looked at my wife with a look that said, "Told you we'd be paying for the extra stuff we're bringing home." Her eyes' response was clear. Charge this expense to experience.

The flight from Manila to Hong Kong was just a warmup. Hong Kong to Vancouver was different. In fact, we utilized our rights as seniors. My wife and I enjoyed our twenty-minute wheelchair service from the Hong Kong arrival gate to the Vancouver departure gate. Hours later, we were adjusting our seat belts and checking out the pillow and blanket provided to each passenger. We prepared our minds and body for the over eleven-hour flight back to Canada.

One of the things we anticipated was the food. Indeed, our breakfast was superb. After four movies, a little chat with my always-sleepy wife, and other channels of entertainment, our plane landed at YVR ten minutes ahead of the arrival time.

The agony began.

We thought our checked-in luggage would be going straight to Calgary. Nope. We had to pick it up and re-check-in at the WestJet counter. I sensed the problem, and my stress climbed up. It took a lot of patience to survive the over thirty-minute line at the immigration clearing area. Just a quick look at my face and then at my passport, and off we went to the moving carousel station. Coming out from the chute was the wrecked cardboard box with the nylon string messed around it. Then came out the three pieces of luggage. We managed to fit all our bags, luggage, and the cardboard box into two carts.

We only had an hour to board our Calgary flight. The distance was long, our carts heavy, bodies tired, and our tummies grumbling loudly. The aura of resignation and despair started to form in my face. My wife sensed it, but we had to move on fast.

There were no people around the departure gate when we reached it. The lady behind the counter insisted that we couldn't bring in the extra small luggage. She put a tag on it and instructed us to just leave the luggage at the door of the plane. We complied.

We were the only ones standing and working our way to our assigned seats. My wife and I, in great relief, looked at each other and at the same time said, "We made it." Minutes later, the plane roared and off we headed for Calgary.

As usual, I ordered cookies and apple juice. My wife ordered pretzels and orange juice. I took a short nap.

LESSON LEARNED

My daughter picked us up at the YYC airport and we reached home early in the evening. The ground was covered with snow and it was minus-twelve degrees Celsius. Indeed, there was no place like home. Home sweet home.

The microwave, air fryer, and the range were all fired up. The table was ready. The leftover food on the table, supplied to my daughter by her aunts while we were on holidays, was the answer to our prayers. In the middle of our meal, my daughter shifted the topic from the best places we'd visited to the lessons we'd learned, insights included.

Our Philippine vacation was the longest time we'd been away from home in the past ten years. In the Philippines, the huge crowd of people traversing the narrow streets made the flow of traffic slow and risky. However, accidents were few and far between. I observed that timing, distance, caution, and cost played a big role in the people's daily routine. Whoever got into the spot or space first, vehicles and people alike, could move ahead. Everyone was aware of the rules of the street. Failure to abide with this norm would cost them lots of time and money. They couldn't afford to be in an accident. The vehicle repair, insurance, medical bills, medicine, and even the legal processes would render a family broke.

The second lesson was that the supply of cheap motorcycles in the market enabled people to move around and establish their livelihood. Not only for pleasure and travel purposes, they also utilized them as the major tool of their trade. The commerce it created put money in the pockets of the people.

Ingenuity and resilience sustained many to climb the economic ladder. Personally, one of the unforgettable lessons we learned concerned the amount of stuff we brought on our holiday. We recognized the dilemma before. Taking more stuff than we could use spelled nuisance and discomfort. This was evidenced by our experience going back home. Not only did we pay dearly, but the physical hassle and wasted time were too much of a burden. If our estimate was right, over half of the clothes we brought weren't used.

Also, the joy of bringing home gifts, like dried goods, candies, and the like, compelled us to buy a big box to contain the same. So aside from the big black luggage, we had to contend with extra loads for check-in at the airport.

Days after our arrival home, I still wasn't fully healed. I had an ear infection that lingered for days, a bad cough that extended for two more weeks, and pink eye for days. The most painful thing, though, was my hole-riddled pockets, the healing of which would take months at least.

That was quite a month-long holiday—refreshing, insightful, and challenging.

THIRD YEAR ANNIVERSARY

March 11, 2022. Over seven million deaths in the world. Humanity panicked. In Canada, total death as of March 6, 2023 was 51,447. So sad. COVID-related mental health issues are dire. Despair lingered still. Millions benefitted from the billions of dollars poured into programs, but my wife had to repay what she'd received.

In Canada, thousands of people lost their jobs, and businesses closed. Families were broken. Mental health issues across the board skyrocketed. People who spewed differing opinions were arrested. Billions of vaccines were manufactured and sold around the world, bringing profits of hundreds of billions of dollars to big pharma. The vaccine claims of stopping transmission and lessening the degree of infection remained debatable. Then came the booster shots. More shots? Nah!

The use of masks, observing distancing, and lockdowns were scientifically and convincingly proven unsatisfactory.

Funny.

Until now, superior minds and authorities in the world haven't figured out where and how the pandemic started. More parliamentary and congressional hearings are held while, silently, COVID is mutating.

The joke is on us. What a three-year Fundemic Moment we had.

News Tidbits

DURING CHAOS LIKE the pandemic, information is the most sought after and important currency. He who has the right and correct information can lead people in the right direction. It can either sway perceptions or change the course of one's decision.

I consume a lot of news every day. In the process, I realize that the news' source may, at times, not be that forthright. No wonder the terms "fake news," "misinformation," "disinformation," and the like spread so quickly.

Excessive news is a reliable source of mental and moral irritation. Sometimes the news is compelling, and unusual news elicits funny thoughts. Below are some of the news items that balanced rage with wit.

Just saying.

VARIANT

Uh-oh! COVID, it's your fault. Even the chaos in Afghanistan copied your mutational capabilities. In 2021, the group that claimed responsibility for the bombing at the airport that killed dozens of US servicemen and scores of Afghans was an ISIS variant—ISIS-K.

OH, SISTER!

Amidst the pandemic, Canadian woman and Gender Equality Minister Maryam Monsef once called the Taliban "brothers." Oh, sister!

KANYE WEST
Kayne posted his new name as Ye. Oh yeah? So what? A new variant—Ye!

RICHEST MAN
In August 2021, Elon Musk, co-founder of Tesla, becomes the world's richest man, worth $186 billion. But his riches don't stop him from eating, sleeping, farting, aging, etc. Oh well, he's no different from us then. A guy with a billion is the same as the other guy with a bunion and vulnerable to COVID infection too.

HOT DOG
One study reported that consuming one hot dog lessens one's life by thirty-six minutes. This was the time I spent waiting for my first jab. And this was the time I saved by not getting a $1.50 hot dog and drink from one of the big box stores in town.

MET GALA
At the peak of the pandemic's fourth wave, the Met Gala in California was held. "Super spreader" was not one of the terms present that night among the attendees. If one had $35,000.00 to spare, MG was a place to display one's vanity. One of the gowns displayed was worn by a US congresswoman. Tax the rich was stitched in red on the back.

Food servers and ushers were all wearing masks, and attendees were oblivious to their borrowed moment of reality. Why would they put COVID masks over their heavily redacted faces? A confusing, hypocritical, and paradoxically weird moment.

What was puzzling about this vanity event was how these creatures wearing elaborate, weirdo attire used the washroom.

MPOX
My down time at the workplace was filled with news reading. The war in Ukraine, China's threat to Taiwan, missile tests by North Korea, the protest in Iran and recently in China. One news item that caught my attention was the renaming of another virus-related disease.

One late afternoon in November, I came across the latest news from the WHO. The world body had changed the name of monkey pox to just "MPox." This was to erase the racial stigma associated with the name.

In my limited understanding, I guess that humans are now afraid of the monkeys. I wonder if soon the earth will be fully inhabited by the apes because of this thinking.

Just saying.

LOCKDOWN PROTEST

The truckers' protest in Ottawa made the government more than nervous, so the *Emergency Act* was invoked for the first time in Canadian history.

Six weeks of testimony by key individuals, including the Prime Minister, ensued. The result may simply be more of the same mind-bending and dramatic rationalization.

Halfway across the world, in China, several cities experienced civil unrest. They not only asked for the cancellation of COVID mandates, but the leaders' hold on power was in jeopardy.

The Canadian Prime Minister had expressed support for the protest in China, but the Chinese protesters had the same goal as the Canadian truckers—let's be done with the COVID mandates.

"Chinada" at its best.

RELIEF SHORTAGE

Months ago, a shortage of baby formula was the big issue. For many weeks, the shortage of cold medication for kids dominated the news in America. In Canada, the shortage of an emergency room beds for sick children was a big concern. The greater problem will be when and if the shortage of diapers materializes.

EIGHT BILLION

The world reached a population milestone—over eight billion people. I'm glad my comprehension is focused and limited most of the time to Dollar Store figures.

TWITTER

It was creating a twister effect. Powerful people were worried. Ordinary people were pensive. The extent of how COVID information was being manipulated will now be exposed. One problem, though: I still don't know how to tweet.

2023 WORD

"Pandemic" was the *Merriam-Webster Dictionary*'s word in 2020. "Vaccine" was the word of 2021, and "gaslighting" in 2022. Gaslighting means "The act or practice of grossly misleading someone, especially for one's own advantage."

There are many popular words vying for 2023. Among them are booster shot, victimhood, racial injustice, residential school, Emergency Act, hypocrite, net zero, climate warrior, COVID protest, inflation, shortages, mental health, reparation, inclusion, equity, diversity, homophobia, misogamist, racist, invasion, cover up, transition, fluidity, cancel, woke, etc. With the increasing craziness in the world, I guess the word then would be "howhy." How and why did it happen?

What about you, my friend. What word you think will stick out in 2023?

DEFINITION

The *Cambridge Dictionary* altered the definition of "woman" and "man." A woman is "an adult who lives and identifies as female, though they may have been said to have a different sex at birth." A man is now defined as "an adult who lives and identifies as male, though they may have been said to have a different sex at birth."

When the pandemic swept around the world, it couldn't care less about the definition of a woman and man. And who cares about Cambridge's altering the definition of words?

FLU

One cold Thursday night in December, I was watching the news. During the pandemic, the worry was the overcrowding of emergency and ICU beds. Thousands of elective surgeries were pushed down the list.

Understaffed and over capacity, units were on the edge of collapse. Then when the flu season set in, the population became more worried. This time it wasn't just about the surge in pandemic infections.

SRV and seasonal flu infections dominated the halls of health care facilities across the land. The young ones were being affected, and the school absentee rate went up. So much stress and pressure rendered our health care professionals exhausted.

The empty pharmacy shelves spoke of how dire the situation was.

I decided that night not to follow the news about COVID, SRV, or the seasonal flu. I took a break and opened our refrigerator. Once I settled my butt on the sofa, the news came on. While I enjoyed my coffee (no sugar), the news focused on the plight of hundreds of thousands of chickens. Avian flu was creeping across the land, and more cases were sprouting up. The government estimated that the dollar damage would reach the hundreds of millions—the same number of chickens that might possibly be buried.

I looked at my wife and said, "I thought we were done with the pandemic. It's hard to cope with the flu and SRV in our children. Now here we are facing another worrying bout of flu."

Would this just be coincidental or nature's fluke?

FTX

One of the biggest frauds in the US mainland was the collapse of FTX, a cryptocurrency company. Billions of dollars were nowhere to be found. As the pandemic was fading from the rearview, the demise of this company rendered thousands of people angry. Endorsed by many prominent people, celebrities, and even politicians, there was nothing they could do to bring back the lost money that had been invested.

The man behind the fiasco was way wealthier than any ordinary bankers. The founder was indeed called the "Bank Man" of cryptocurrency. For reasons only known to him, after a series of bad decisions, his name was "fried" alive by the media.

Pandemic, vaccine, cryptocurrency—these were the issues that greatly impacted the world.

Just saying.

GOBLIN MODE

This term refers to "a type of behavior which is unapologetically self-indulgent, lazy, slovenly, or greedy, typically in a way that rejects social norms or expectations," according to *Oxford Dictionary*, which named it the official word of 2022.

Gaslighting and goblin mode are like social consequences of the pandemic. Misleading others to reject social norms was one of the worst social ills in the pandemic.

I keep myself mindful of this stuff so that I won't be gaslighted and gobbled.

PLASTIC

The end of 2022 brought the end of single use plastic products, especially shopping bags, in Canada. When I heard the news, I went to the kitchen and opened one of the pantries. Crumpled and tucked in it were about thirty plastic bags from various stores. Under the sink, a black garbage bin overflowed with the same item. I knew downstairs there were more around. I was confident these plastic bags would last through another year of use. Ironically, though, every time we went shopping, we forgot to bring plastic bags. So we ended up paying extra.

One day we realized it would be more practical to just grab empty cardboard boxes inside the store where we shopped. This way we were helping the store get rid of the boxes. There were no more plastic bags, and we helped the recycling company collect more items from our blue garbage bin. However, we kept sturdy-looking boxes for future storage use. Indeed, many items that we seldom use are stored in these cardboard boxes, along with unused sanitizers, boxes of masks, wipes, gloves, test kits, and other related health and safety items.

Unknowingly, we added new items on top of the existing pile of stuff lying around and occupied a chunk of space in the house.

Single use plastic could be eliminated, but the consequence deserved another look. The production of cardboard and recyclable materials would entail more energy to produce.

It was like taking a vaccine when nobody knew the long-term side effects.

FOOLISH

Musk will step down if he finds someone foolish enough for the job. Who would argue that there is no fun in this social media. Only fools rush to conclusions.

Twit, tweet, and tweak …

BALLOON

Just days after our return from the Philippines, the North American news was dominated by the Chinese balloon flying over Canada and US air space. The size of three school buses, the balloon would be shot down only after it was deemed safe to do so. The safety of civilians was the priority. Days later, the flying object was shot down over South Carolina.

The news didn't stop. Another one was spotted over the northern part of Canada. It took days also before it was downed by NORAD. The reason for the delay was probably to protect the bear population in Yukon territory. NORAD was still monitoring several balloons in the area.

Couldn't it be just stray balloons from Chinese New Year and/or balloon festival celebrations?

LAB LEAK

Information about the origin of the COVID pandemic has circled back, and the lab leak theory has gained traction. I guess what we all need now is not only distancing but ear plugs. Distancing from news and ear plugs to block depressing news and chatter. We have the choice to decide for our own benefit. The pandemic taught us so many things.

INTERNATIONAL WOMEN'S DAY 2023

The first lady of the U.S.A. honoured a transgender woman (biological man) on this day. The awardee felt, identified, and proclaimed himself as a woman. He advocated for the cause of the LQBGT community. The more attention given to people transitioning than to real women only demeans and dilutes the meaning and essence of womanhood. Where art thou, feminists?

How can Americans celebrate Women's Day if most of their leaders don't know what a woman is?

FUNNY!

In Canada, the same degree of attention and appreciation was given to transgender people during International Women's Day. I wonder if and how COVID affected the mind, logic, morality, and rationality of human beings.

Your guess is as good as mine.

WOKE HOUSE

Many people would say that Canada and the US are systemic racist countries. When we immigrated to Canada over thirty years ago, the issue of racism was a hot social issue. In the south, the matter was so intense. Their daily news reflected it all.

Memorials and statues of founding fathers have been toppled down. Cancelling culture has become a fad. The lens of equity, inclusion, and diversity has become the yardstick and standard of the government's operation.

The disdain for White people is paramount. It even came from the White president, whose official abode is called the White House. I would suspect with humour that anti-racist groups forgot to notice this. Why not change the official name of the residence of the president to the "Woke House"?

I wouldn't blame COVID for this, for sure.

What Now?

THE JOURNEY TO full recovery and normalcy was arduous, and clouds of uncertainty are still hanging up there. Coupled with the world's current events, the future seems headed for unfamiliar and dangerous terrain. The regional conflicts in Europe and brewing instability in Asia dampen the remaining hope for the future. The election south of the border, inflation, and so many social issues pull many to despair, hopelessness, and helplessness.

Until now, the debate about the vaccine's ability to stop transmission was in question. Even the origin of the virus is still the hot issue in the world. One study reported that there are more vaccinated people dying of COVID infections: "In a startling revelation, a Washington Post analysis has found that more vaccinated people are now dying of the Covid disease and 58 per cent of coronavirus deaths in August in the US 'were people who were vaccinated or boosted'."[1]

For the first time since the beginning of the pandemic in early 2020, many Americans dying from COVID were at least partially vaccinated, according to the new analysis of federal and state data: "In September 2021, vaccinated people made up just 23 per cent of coronavirus fatalities. In January and February this year, it was up to 42 per cent," the report mentioned.[2]

---

[1] "Vaccinated People Now Make Majority of Covid Deaths in US: Report," Business Standard, November 24, 2022, https://www.business-standard.com/article/international/vaccinated-people-now-make-majority-of-covid-deaths-in-us-report-122112400391_1.html.

[2] Ibid.

So what do we take from this? There is so much to learn from this twenty-first- century epic disruption in human history. To name a few:

Relationship. Life is short, and COVID acted like a passport. My relationship with my wife, children, relatives, friends, colleagues, neighbours, and associates has morphed into a more serious consideration. The need to reconnect and engage with loved ones is more compelling than ever before, even with a friend that owed me not only gratitude but also a garden tool he'd borrowed years back. He needed to be reminded of the tool and my great concern for him too.

COVID levels off the rough edges of friendship too. Everyone wishes for good health and long life. In the ocean of the pandemic, no man is an island, indeed.

Responsibility. Health and safety are everyone's responsibility. It took me almost three years to condition and convince myself to be tidier and healthier every day. I wanted my dealings with my dear ones to be closer, deeper, more pleasant, transparent, more meaningful, and refreshing. Because what matters most to me then and now is a healthy relationship with these folks.

Since then, I seldom miss my maintenance pills for my diabetes. Regrettably, I forgot my Metformin when we had our fifteen-day out-of-the-country holiday in October.

Resources. COVID's impact on the economy and financial wellbeing of people was severe. Thousands were added to the ranks of unemployed. COVID became the silent and active partner of this predicament. Personal debt was astronomical. The government relief fund was just a Band-Aid solution. The economy was picking up, yet substantial relief was still far off. The price of food went through the roof. Affordability became a big issue for less fortunate sectors. I wondered if I could afford a new toothbrush every month.

Relentless. The pandemic was relentless. It didn't respect anyone. The impact was felt from womb to tomb. Vaccine manufacturers seemed to be aware of this opportunity, and jabs were available for babies to oldies and in between. Even for domesticated animals and family pets, the COVID vaccine might become a common requirement.

Covid made age arbitrary. It made me felt good about myself. No one could boast about one's age advantage. From a wobbly and stooping walk to a springy and bubbling stroll, all were vulnerable to the disease. COVID was a very reliable life equalizer.

Route. Online ordering became the fad. Virtually anything can be ordered online and delivered efficiently. Fewer people shop in-store now due to health protocols and hassles, and inflation is keeping people from spending. Yet the route to this trend is paved with promise and more opportunities.

Private, small, and start-up delivery services compete fiercely with the big boys. Cost, efficiency, and quality became the standard everyone is trying to surpass, the benefits of which trickle down to the consuming populace.

My daughter was eager to teach me how to place an app on my cell phone. A new route for me to make the life of a senior more enjoyable and less stressful. Now the pressing issue that stresses me is how to work the app.

Rearrange. Working from home became normal during the pandemic. At the onset, I couldn't be part of this trend. My work's tasks entailed the use of office equipment and in-person dealing with clients. I was envious of the many who were even given an allowance to renovate part of their abode for this purpose.

I guess COVID designed itself to alter most of our whereabouts and what abouts. It was good and effective at rearranging the physical and work environment of the working masses. I was with the minority, stuck in my workplace for over twenty-nine years.

Reservation. In a span of three years, humanity was faced with various conflicting and often vague information. For the first few months into the pandemic, people had great trust in the government and public health officials. It seemed that everyone, out of fear, followed all directives without question. Then came some realizations. Infections persisted. Transmission was not abetted. Vaccine efficacy was under question. Health directives were being ignored. The threat of arrest and economic consequences ramped up.

Reservation came into play. Now things coming from the authorities were taken with a grain of salt. People became smarter. Google and social media helped people see all sides of the picture. More questions were raised and less answers given. Just follow. Period.

The pandemic validated the importance of reservation. More people were coming to view the pandemic as a tool for accumulating more power. Those who expressed their reservations about government mandates were treated less favourably. I belonged to the camp of "reservationists." No wonder my wife and daughter seldom agree with me.

Regrouping. The period of health mandate compliance resulted in a dynamic change in our interactions with the people around us, including our family members. It seemed distance was hard to let go of. Hence, even in formal and informal meetings we were accustomed to keeping some distance from others, especially from those with whom we have little familiarity. Over time, however, the regrouping of people was moving back to normal.

Resurgence. The resurgence of human activities manifested life and society's emergence from cruel isolation. Many ignored health mandated protocols, and the government was unable to stop the flow and power of the people exercising freedom. Mask wearing became a joke. Distancing turned into a menacing habit.

People and communities were exploring the atmosphere and environment to re-enact and re-live the life they missed so dearly during the pandemic. At the end of it all, there's one thing humanity can always resort to. Laughter remains and will always be the best medicine.

Fundemic Moments.

As scripture says …

There is a time for everything, and a season for every activity under the heavens:

a time to be born and a time to die, a time to plant and a time to uproot,

a time to kill and a time to heal, a time to tear down and a time to build, a time to weep *and a time to laugh*, a time to mourn *and a time to dance*,

a time to scatter stones and a time to gather them, a time to embrace and a time to refrain

from embracing,

a time to search and a time to give up, a time to keep and a time to throw away,

a time to tear and a time to mend, a time to be silent and a time to speak,

a time to love and a time to hate, a time for war and a time for peace.

What do workers gain from their toil? I have seen the burden God has laid on the human race. He has made everything beautiful in its time. He has also set eternity in the human heart; yet no one can fathom what God has done from beginning to end. (Ecclesiastes 3:1–11, NIV, emphasis added)

COVID's time has passed. Our time to reflect and face life at its best is here. Have fun and be content with it.

"A happy heart is good medicine and a cheerful mind works healing, but a broken spirit dries up the bones" (Proverbs 17:22, AMPC; see also Proverbs 12:25, 15:13, 15)

IMAGES TAKEN DURING THE PANDEMIC

A week after the pandemic was declared.

Calgary's three brothers under the weather.

No one told me about lockdown and isolation.

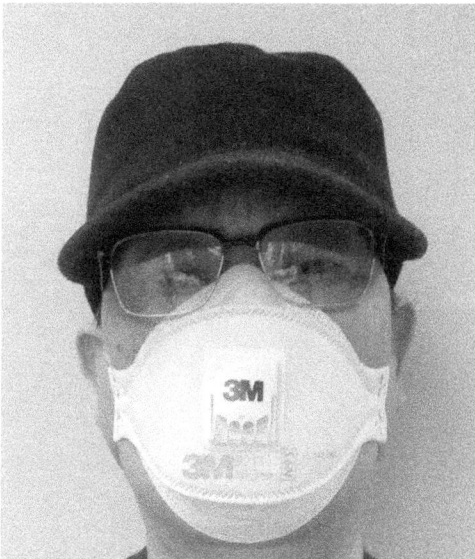

My first mask.

Early sign of pandemic defiance.

Our lunch room's bulletin board during the pandemic.

Porta pets. Our loyal and worry-free holiday companions.

TreeBute to Covid 19 Pandemic Heroes. Elliston Park, Calgary, AB, Canada.

Suddenly they are all wearing masks.

COVID 19 FUNDEMIC SELECTED SKETCHES

Earth is chaotic and a risky place. We need this one.

Vaccine for us. Oh, no!

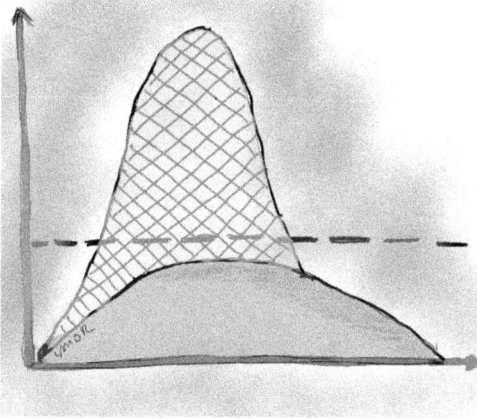

Netted - Flatten the curve. Gray - lessen the carb.

The unmasked salon patron.

Folks, we can't tik tok. No wifi signal.

How the pandemic changed our view.

Unproven origin of the pandemic.

The trend setter.

About the Author

ROMEO IS A FILIPINO-Canadian author who has resided in Alberta, Canada for over thirty years with his wife and children.

His first book, *Open Visa*, was published over a decade ago. The book highlights the inspiring, encouraging, and challenging life stories of Filipino overseas foreign workers and caregivers. The positive reviews it received created a following in the community.

In mid-2020, he penned and published *Covid-19 Fundemic*. This journal-type book was dedicated to all COVID-19 pandemic heroes. During the pandemic, people have a choice to feel desperate, anxious, and hopeless. Or they can focus on what makes life more bearable, light, and appreciative of funny moments. As suggested in the book, Romeo initiated the declaration of COVID-19 Pandemic Heroes Day on December 21, 2020, in Alberta. Since then, with the generous support of businesses and organizations, over 2,750 COVID heroes have received certificates of recognition/appreciation and gift bags.

As the current Chair of Diaryo Alberta Society, Romeo conceived and directed the Society's publication of a monthly newsletter called *Miscellanews* and an event-specific magazine called *Allbertans*.

Romeo has worked at many jobs over the years as a researcher, speaker, facilitator, consultant, and contributor to local community papers, such as *Diaryo Alberta* in Calgary, *Alberta Filipino Journal* in Edmonton, and *Taliba* newspaper in Toronto, Ontario.

He's an avid gardener in the summer (ha ha ha), and occasionally a poet and composer. By popular demand, he's a chauffeur for his wife and family.

By occupation, Romeo is a grain inspector with the Canadian Grain Commission.

www.ingramcontent.com/pod-product-compliance
Lightning Source LLC
Chambersburg PA
CBHW020158090426
42734CB00008B/863

9 7 8 1 4 8 6 6 2 4 5 8 4